ESSENCE OF THE BHAGAVAD GITA

Essence of the
BHAGAVAD GITA

A Contemporary Guide to Yoga,

Meditation & Indian Philosophy

EKNATH EASWARAN

First printed November 2011
ISBN : 978–1–58638–068–7 (paperback)
ISBN : 978–1–58638–029–8 (hardcover)
ISBN : 978–1–58638–069–4 (ebook)

Publisher's Cataloging-In-Publication Data
(Prepared by The Donohue Group, Inc.)
Easwaran, Eknath, 1910-1999.
    Essence of the Bhagavad Gita : a contemporary guide to
yoga, meditation & Indian philosophy / Eknath Easwaran.
    p. ; cm. -- (Wisdom of India ; bk. 2)
    Includes A garland of verses, a selection of verses
translated by Eknath Easwaran.
    Issued also as an ebook.
    Includes bibliographical references and index.
    ISBN : 978–1–58638–068–7
    1. Bhagavadgita--Criticism, interpretation, etc. 2.
Spiritual life--Hinduism. 3. Yoga. 4. Meditation--
Hinduism. 5. Indian philosophy. I. Title. II. Series: Wisdom
of India (Tomales, Calif.) ; bk. 2.
BL1138.66 .E57   294.5/924   2011   922429

Nilgiri Press is the publishing division of the
Blue Mountain Center of Meditation, a nonprofit
organization founded by Eknath Easwaran in 1961.
www.bmcm.org | info@bmcm.org

The Blue Mountain Center of Meditation
Box 256, Tomales, California 94971
Telephone: +1 707 878 2369 | 800 475 2369

◇ Table of Contents

This book has been produced by Eknath Easwaran's senior editors, longtime students who worked closely with him since his first book in 1970 and were charged by him with continuing to compile his books from transcripts of his talks after his passing.

In his last editorial planning meeting, in 1998, Easwaran gave instructions about the books in progress that he wanted completed from his unpublished transcripts, outlines, and notes. Essence of the Bhagavad Gita *is the first of those posthumous projects to be published, Easwaran's final distillation of the Gita's teachings. It is something rare and precious: the legacy of a gifted teacher sharing a lifetime's immersion in a sacred text, conveyed in his talks and informal sessions with some of his closest students.*

It is a great privilege to pass such a work as this on to Easwaran's readers around the world.

◇ *The Wisdom of India*

SOME YEARS AGO I translated what I called the classics of Indian spirituality: the Upanishads, the Bhagavad Gita, and the Dhammapada. These ancient texts, memorized and passed from generation to generation for hundreds of years before they were written down, represent early chapters in the long, unbroken story of India's spiritual experience. The Upanishads, old before the dawn of history, come to us like snapshots of a timeless landscape. The Gita condenses and elaborates on these insights in a dialogue set on a battlefield, as apt a setting now as it was three thousand years ago. And the Dhammapada, a kind of spiritual handbook, distills the practical implications of the same truths presented afresh by the Compassionate Buddha around 500 B.C.

These translations proved surprisingly popular, perhaps because they were intended not so much to be literal or literary as to bring out the meaning of these documents for us today. For it is here that these classics come to life. They are not dry texts; they speak to us. Each is the opening voice of a conversation which we are invited to join – a voice that expects a reply. So in India we say that the meaning of the scriptures is only complete when this call is answered in the lives of men and women like you and me. Only then do we see what the scriptures mean here and now. G. K. Chesterton once said that to understand the Gospels, we have only to look at St. Francis of Assisi. Similarly, I would say, to grasp the meaning of the Bhagavad Gita, we need look no farther than Mahatma Gandhi, who made it a guide for every aspect of daily living. Wisdom may be perennial, but to see its relevance we must see it lived out.

In India, this process of assimilating the learning of the head into the wisdom of the heart is said to have three stages: *shravanam, mananam,* and *nididhyasanam;* roughly, hearing, reflection, and meditation. These steps can merge naturally into a single daily activity, but they can also be steps in a journey that unfolds over years. Often this journey is begun in response to a crisis. In my own case, though I must have heard the scriptures many times as a child, I don't remember them making any deep impression. When I discovered the Bhagavad Gita, I was attracted by the beauty of its poetry; I didn't understand its teachings at all. It was not until I reached a crisis of meaning in my mid-thirties, when outward success failed to fill the longing in my heart, that I turned to these classics for wisdom rather than literary beauty. Only then did

I see that I had been, as the Buddha puts it, like a spoon that doesn't know the taste of the soup.

Since that time I have dedicated myself to translating these scriptures into daily living through the practice of meditation. The book in your hands is one fruit of this long endeavor. Such a presentation can only be intensely personal. In my translations I naturally let the texts speak for themselves; here I make no attempt to hide the passion that gave those translations their appeal. To capture the essence of the Gita, the Upanishads, and the Dhammapada, I offer what I have learned personally from trying to live them out in a complex, hurried world. I write not as a scholar, but as an explorer back from a long, long voyage eager to tell what he has found.

Yet however personal the exploration, these discoveries are universal. So it is not surprising that at the heart of each of these classics lies a myth – variations on the age-old story of a hero in quest of wisdom that will redeem the world. In the Upanishads, a teenager goes to the King of Death to find the secret of immortality. In the Gita, standing between opposing armies on the eve of Armageddon, the warrior-prince Arjuna seeks guidance from an immortal teacher, Sri Krishna. And behind the Dhammapada lies the story of the Buddha himself, a true story woven into legend: a prince who forsakes his throne to find a way for all the world to go beyond sorrow in this life. These old stories are our own, as relevant today as ever. Myth always involves the listener. We identify with its heroes; their crises mirror ours. Their stories remind us not only what these scriptures mean but why they matter. Like the texts themselves, they seek a response in our own lives.

So this book is both the fruit of a journey and an invitation. If you like, you may read it as a traveler's tale rich in the experience of some distant place, enjoying the sights and adventures without the travail of actually making the trip yourself. But this place is really no more distant than the heart, so if you find that this description calls you to your own voyage of exploration, my highest purpose in writing will be fulfilled.

◇ *Introduction*

THE BHAGAVAD GITA is India's best-known scripture – magnificent poetry couched as a dialogue between a warrior-prince named Arjuna and his charioteer and teacher, Sri Krishna, an avatar of God – that is, God in human form. The dialogue form is important, for the Gita is not a book of commandments but a book of choices. Arjuna, a man of action, turns to Sri Krishna in a crisis of confusion about how to act; Sri Krishna presents the highest wisdom and then leaves it to Arjuna to decide – an element of freedom that is a major part of the Gita's appeal to readers today.

I can't remember when my love of the Gita began. As a child I had no conscious interest in anything spiritual; I was an ordinary boy growing up in a remote South Indian village, absorbed in my friends and pets and our sports and games. But one summer before I reached the age of ten, my grandmother decided that instead of swimming and playing soccer,

I should spend my vacations learning Sanskrit from the village priest. I learned in the traditional manner, year after year, from passages committed to memory from India's great scriptures and poets – including many verses from the Bhagavad Gita. The poetry appealed to me deeply, but so far as I can tell the words must have sunk into my unconscious without any sense of their deeper meaning. Only years later, through the example of Mahatma Gandhi, did I begin to understand the Gita as not only magnificent literature, but a sure guide to human affairs – a guide that could, in fact, throw light on the problems I faced in my own times of crisis.

Religion as Realization

Sarvepalli Radhakrishnan, the second president of India and a profound scholar, once commented that the ancient Greeks gave the world intellectual values, the Romans political values, and the Jews moral values. India's contribution, he added, is spiritual values. It is a generalization, but one with a good deal of truth. A civilization can be evaluated by the kind of human being it aims at, the highest ideal it holds up. Wherever we look in India's long history, we find the highest honor given to men and women dedicated to the realization of the supreme reality that most religions call God.

I think it was Arnold Toynbee, in the course of his study of world civilizations, who said that India had a genius for religion: not in the sense of a particular religion, but religion itself.

This needs some explanation, for we are used to thinking of religions in the plural, bound to particular cultures, and thus of India's scriptures as Hindu. But the word *Hinduism,* even the idea, does not appear in our scriptures, and it is really too narrow to describe what India means by religion. The term that is used is *sanatana dharma. Sanatana* means changeless, eternal; *dharma* is a rich and complex word that we can translate here as law. Sanatana dharma is the bedrock of reality, the eternal principles or changeless values on which life is based, regardless of creed, country, culture, or epoch.

The oldest expression of this idea goes back a good five thousand years to the cradle of Indian mysticism, the Upanishads – visionary records of the direct encounters of anonymous sages with a transcendent reality. The Upanishads are lofty and inspiring, but they are not terribly practical: they tell what sages have found, but little about how others can make this discovery themselves. Yet the whole point of sanatana dharma is that religion must be based on personal experience. We need some way to translate the wisdom of the Upanishads into living, daily reality.

That is where the Bhagavad Gita scores heavily. In the Gita, the wisdom of the Upanishads is complemented and brought to earth by Sri Krishna, who, through Arjuna, tells us – you and me – what practices to follow to gain direct, experiential knowledge of reality. In Indian philosophy, the various paths to this wisdom are called *yoga* and the underlying theory is *sankhya.* At some point in the development of Indian thought – perhaps early in the first millennium B.C. – sankhya and the major schools of yoga became systematized. But the Gita was composed much earlier, while these schools of thought were still emerging. As a result, it is broad enough to support all paths that lead to the discovery of sanatana dharma, examining them not systematically but in dialogue – a major virtue, for dialogue naturally accommodates various points of view and rewards exploration. This allows the Gita to be inclusive rather than dogmatic, with the result that virtually every major philosophical system in India refers to the Gita for authority.

One aspect of this relatively early stage of Indian mysticism can be frustrating to a modern reader: terms and ideas commingle without rigorous boundaries or definitions. The sages who gave us the Upanishads and Bhagavad Gita do not seem to have been philosophically inclined; they chose to sing rather than define, with the result that a key word such as *yoga* is used in the Gita in different ways. The idea is that the meaning of such words is so full that the best way to get at it is to consider it in a living context from various points of view, the way one makes a map from the observations of several travelers. In this book, rather than serve up one of the later definitions of such words and narrow their meaning, it has seemed best to approach them as they are used and allow the meaning to build up as understanding deepens.

With one major exception, I shall also ignore later commentaries in order to focus on the Bhagavad Gita itself and what I have learned from it personally. The exception is certain key words and ideas introduced by a towering eighth-century mystic from South India named Shankara, whose brilliant commentaries on the Upanishads and Bhagavad Gita established the canon of Indian mysticism. Some of these ideas – particularly the doctrine of *maya,* the illusion of separateness – appear in the Gita but are not elaborated; Shankara's explanations are simply too insightful to be ignored.

The Epic Setting

The Bhagavad Gita appears in the sixth book of an immense epic called the *Mahabharata,* which tells the story of the struggle between two rival branches of the same dynasty: the Pandavas, five brothers, and the Kauravas, their cousins. But this story is only the backbone of the *Mahabharata.* India's oral tradition, like India itself, is syncretic, and over the centuries many, many other stories and bits of mythology, lore, and wisdom were grafted onto this main storyline. The *Mahabharata* is not so much a single work as a literature in itself. Though it can be condensed into a running narrative, the vast majority of us in India absorb it in pieces, episodes that are told or sung or dramatized on their own.

The Bhagavad Gita is one of these independent episodes and seems to have been always considered a work of its own. It is not so much part of the *Mahabharata* as an Upanishad, slipped into the narrative about a third of the way in – a view supported by the traditional colophon that ends each chapter, which identifies the Gita as an Upanishad on yoga.

So far as drama goes, in any case, the Gita's placement in the storyline is brilliant. Despite attempts by the Pandavas to preserve peace, the Kauravas have insisted on war – a cataclysmic conflict that will draw in almost every kingdom in India. The Gita begins on the morning before battle is joined. Arjuna, one of the Pandavas, instructs his charioteer, Sri Krishna, to drive their chariot into the open field between the opposing armies. There, seeing family, friends, and teachers preparing to destroy one another, he throws his bow to the ground and tells Krishna he cannot go on.

At this point the story is suspended, and we are lifted out of time while Sri Krishna gives Arjuna comprehensive instruction in the essentials of life and death: the Bhagavad Gita. Then the teaching concludes, we drop back into the narrative, and the *Mahabharata* continues – thousands upon thousands of verses giving the tragic details of a convulsive eighteen-day war in which virtually all the major combatants on both sides compromise their honor and are slain.

It is simplest, of course, to see the Gita as an integral part of this story, an episode that needs no explanation. Yet its overall character is so different from what comes before and after that it is easy to see why instead it has often been considered an allegory. The names themselves encourage this: the battlefield – Kurukshetra, "the field of the Kuru dynasty" – is dubbed *dharma-kshetra,* "the field of righteousness"; King Dhritarashtra's name can mean "he who has usurped the throne"; the names of his sons all begin with *du-,* "evil," and their eldest, Duryodhana – literally "dirty fighter" – leaves us no doubt about how well his name fits. On the other side is Sri Krishna, no less than an incarnation of God, and Arjuna and his four brothers, each of whom has a god as his father. While things are never quite black and white – the *Mahabharata* is as complex as Shakespeare – no one has ever wondered who the "good guys" are, or doubted that this war is a struggle between good and evil.

Mahatma Gandhi took this a step further: the war the Gita describes, he held, actually takes place within ourselves. There *is* a field called Kurukshetra north of Delhi where this battle is said to have taken place, but in Gandhi's view the real battlefield is one's own life, where the struggle between right and wrong, good and evil, rages from birth to death. There is ample support for this view in the text itself: for example, when Sri Krishna tells Arjuna that the enemies he must conquer are lust, fear, and anger. The dialogue between these two then becomes not so much symbolic as a searching of the soul – an interpretation that becomes living truth when one tries to translate the Gita's teachings into thought and action. Like so many other dialogues between God and man in mystical literature East and West – *The Imitation of Christ,* the Psalms of

David, the Katha Upanishad, the writings of Heinrich Suso or of Mechthild of Magdeburg – this is the heart's appeal for wisdom and guidance, answered, as it only can be, from within. Then the choice of a dialogue format may remind us of Plato: the wisdom is within us, not in the text; the Gita only serves to draw it out.

One last point brings the Bhagavad Gita directly into our times. The central message of the Gita is that life is an indivisible whole – a concept that contemporary civilization flouts at every turn. Until we learn the principles of unity and how to live in harmony with them, the Gita would say, we cannot have abiding peace or live in harmony with each other and the planet; we cannot even enjoy the real and lasting progress that is the hallmark of civilization.

The Gita doesn't ask us to take this on faith. It simply offers a frame of reference through which we can look afresh at what we see around us, scrutinize the plans and promises offered by contemporary politics and economics, and judge for ourselves how useful any approach can be that does not begin with the essential unity of life.

◇

ESSENCE OF THE BHAGAVAD GITA

PROLOGUE

CLOSE YOUR EYES. *You have been blind like this from birth, ruler of a kingdom you cannot see, dependent on the advice of those around you, some wise, most otherwise. Your choices of whom to listen to and whom to ignore have led to a war that will end in ruin for both sides. Unable to watch the pending catastrophe with your own eyes, you appeal to your charioteer, who possesses extrasensory vision:*

> *Tell me, Sanjaya, what is happening on the field of battle, the field of dharma, where my army and my enemies have gathered for war. (1:1)*

So the Bhagavad Gita begins, with the words of the blind king Dhritarashtra, whose crippling attachment to his selfish sons has split his dynasty in two.

This is also the last we shall hear from him, for the Gita has very little to do with his story or his war. Yet this opening verse makes a haunting introduction to the theme of a war within, and Dhritarashtra's plight is a sobering reminder that each of us, too, has probably made blind decisions that have left us perplexed about how we got here and how to face a future that we ourselves have helped to create.

Clearing up this confusion is the purpose of the Gita, so we shall spend no more time with blind kings and their stories. It is not Dhritarashtra who stands for us but Arjuna, a warrior who seeks understanding of life, death, and duty from his charioteer, Sri Krishna, a divine incarnation who has chosen him as his disciple and friend. Like Dhritarashtra, we too are about to listen in on a hidden dialogue, not one far away but deep within the heart. And while we too are unable to watch, the Gita will let us hear – and, more important, help us to understand.

◇ *The War Within*

WE OPEN THE Gita and are plunged into the confusion of war. Armies are about to clash, and the air echoes with the blare of conch horns and the trumpeting of elephants in full armor – pandemonium that surely belongs more to the *Iliad* or even a war movie than to a scripture on yoga.

Yet this drama is essentially stage-setting – a bridge to the real beginning of the Bhagavad Gita in chapter 2, when Sri Krishna begins to teach. Then we find ourselves in a different world, serene and detached, where verse after verse reveals that the battle referred to is one that takes place within: the struggle between right and wrong, selfishness and selflessness, anger and compassion, that rages continuously in every human heart. The chaos of the opening chapter only mirrors the turmoil we feel within.

Each of us can recognize Arjuna's crisis here, caught as he

is between opposing forces in a struggle beyond his control. With reason and duty pleading for both sides, he is pulled in two, so unsure of what is right that he cannot act:

ARJUNA:

O Krishna, I see my own relations here anxious to fight, and my limbs grow weak; my mouth is dry, my body shakes, and my hair is standing on end. My skin burns, and the bow Gandiva has slipped from my hand. I am unable to stand; my mind seems to be whirling. These signs bode evil for us. . . .

SANJAYA:

Overwhelmed by sorrow, Arjuna spoke these words. Casting away his bow and his arrows, he sat down in his chariot in the middle of the battlefield.

(1:28, 47)

Much of this struggle is hidden from our conscious awareness. We may glimpse it in dreams or therapy sessions, but we have learned to close our eyes and pretend it does not exist. We see only its consequences, the painful wastage of conflict and indecision that litters our days: the skirmishes of daily life, quarrels at home and work, angry outbursts at those we love, absurd tensions that we can neither explain nor set aside. Turbulent thoughts urge us in opposing directions, undermining the will, leaving us doubtful and confused about what to do. This may not be Ypres or Stalingrad, but the fight is epic enough – and, like the Hundred Years War, it can last a lifetime.

All the confusion in our daily lives, the Gita teaches, arises from this turmoil in the mind. Uncertain about what to do, we end up fighting on both sides. We are fighting ourselves, and the conflict lays waste our strength.

And the turmoil is contagious. Anger and suspicion spread. All conflicts in the world outside us, the Gita would say – not just our own small battles, but those that divide communities and even nations – are the sum total of the internal conflicts raging around the globe. The wars, persecutions, and violence that fuel the morning news do not erupt out of nowhere, but depend on ordinary people fanning the flames of hatred, fear, and anger. As the Buddha puts it, everyone is on fire, and little is required for us to fan each other into a blaze. At home and work, just one person getting angry can set fire to everyone around; while on the international level, the world has seen far too many instances where people who have lived together for generations suddenly break out in savage violence or civil war.

Higher & Lower Self

Underlying this confusion, the Gita would say, is a kind of schizophrenia. We don't know who we are. We don't know what we are as human beings, so we are divided against ourselves. On the one hand, we behave like separate creatures engaged in a struggle for survival with the rest of life. Yet at some deep level, we also know that this image of ourselves is inaccurate: that we are not separate from nature but part of a much larger whole, motivated not merely by personal survival but even more by love, ideals, beauty, a sense of right and wrong – values that can't be denied without losing something of our humanity.

That is why Arjuna's plea for help at the outset of the Gita – so immediate, so personal, so urgent – is met by a reply that is lofty, universal, and timeless

SRI KRISHNA:

You speak sincerely, but your sorrow has no cause. The wise grieve neither for the living nor for the dead. There has never been a time when you and I and the kings gathered here have not existed, nor will there be a time when we will cease to exist. . . .

The impermanent has no reality; reality lies in the eternal. Those who have seen the boundary between these two have attained the end of all knowledge. Realize that which pervades the universe and is indestructible; no power can affect this unchanging, imperishable reality.

The body is mortal, but that which dwells in the
body is immortal and immeasurable. . . . You were
never born; you will never die. You have never
changed; you can never change. Unborn, eternal,
immutable, immemorial, you do not die when the body
dies. (2:11–12, 16–20)

Under the circumstances, this reply sounds hopelessly philosophical. Arjuna is in a crisis that is about to explode, with disastrous consequences; he wants to know what to *do.* We may feel
similarly impatient facing our own crises. Yet instead of hacking
at branches, the Gita is going to the root. If we don't know who
we are, we can't know what we want and will go on seeking
things that can't satisfy us, ultimately at the expense of anyone
who gets in the way. At first this leads merely to frustration, but
frustration leads to anger and anger can build up to war. Only by
understanding who we are and what can truly satisfy us can we
find a basis for living together in peace and prosperity.

The Gita presents this dilemma as a conflict between a lower self and a higher one. The Sanskrit word for what makes us
identify with this lower, separate self is *ahamkara* – literally,
"I-maker," the component of personality that presents us to
ourselves as isolated from the rest of life. Calling this self
"lower" simply reflects the fact that it is so limited – just the
slimmest fraction of what we are as human beings. Compared
with what we really are, the Gita says, this lesser self is a cage
of separateness, and identifying ourselves with it is the source

of insecurity, friction, disrupted relationships, and mounting dissatisfaction.

In practical terms, as long as there is division in consciousness, there will be separateness simply because this is how we see: "People are other than me; it's me against the world." And as long as there is separateness, there will always be a tendency to exploit and manipulate others to make up for what we feel we lack.

We can envision this division in consciousness as a wound that never heals. In a few people this wound is only skin-deep: the sense of separateness is slight, so they are secure and do not depend on anything outside themselves; they are sensitive to the needs of others without needing to lean on anyone. But most of us suffer from a cut in consciousness that goes to the bone; and the deeper the cut, the greater the insecurity that comes from feeling isolated from the rest of life and even from oneself. From this insecurity comes conflict and all the other negative emotions and behavior that arise from feeling alienated and alone: frustration, depression, loneliness, jealousy, suspicion, resentment, acquisitiveness, anger. Worst, each of these effects becomes a cause; they interconnect and feed each other, as chaotic as the weather, building to a storm.

In other words, this split in consciousness conditions how we see life. So long as we see through the conditioning of separateness, life seems fragments of a puzzle that do not fit together, without even a picture on the box.

How shall we characterize this split? It has been called a tug of war between the selfish and the selfless in us, a tension between a higher self and a lower one, a struggle between wisdom and ignorance of our real nature. More positively, we can think of it as the tension of an evolutionary drive towards the full realization of our human potential. According to the Gita, in every one of us – by virtue of our being human – there is an upward surge to evolve, to grow in humanity day by day, and a downward pull to remain engaged in conflict as separate creatures set against the rest of life. In this view, the human being is still in the making, evolving from an animal past towards a much greater freedom. The war within is between the inertia of our biological heritage and this irrepressible drive to fulfill what is latent in our nature.

Sri Aurobindo, one of the most profound mystics of the twentieth century, captures this idea in an epic poem called *Savitri,* the theme of which is the human being's emergence from an evolutionary past into unconditioned freedom. Here are just a few lines describing the human condition as "a link between the demigod and the beast":

> He knows not his own greatness nor his aim;
> He has forgotten why he has come and whence;
> His spirit and his members are at war . . .
> All sides he sees and turns to every call;
> He has no certain light by which to walk;

His life is a blind-man's-buff, a hide and seek;
He seeks himself and from himself he runs. . . .

"His spirit and his members are at war." Here is the language of the battlefield again, and the Gita makes it clear what our enemies are: all that is violent in us, all that is selfish, all that is hostile, all that is unkind.

ARJUNA:

What is the force that binds us to selfish deeds, O Krishna? What power moves us, even against our will, as if forcing us?

SRI KRISHNA:

It is selfish desire and anger . . . these are the appetites and evils that threaten a person in this life. Just as a fire is covered by smoke and a mirror is obscured by dust, just as the embryo rests deep within the womb, knowledge is hidden by selfish desire – hidden, Arjuna, by this unquenchable fire for self-satisfaction, the inveterate enemy of the wise. . . .

Fight with all your strength, Arjuna! Controlling your senses, conquer your enemy, the destroyer of knowledge and realization. (3:36–39, 41)

Why do we cling to such a narrow, conditioned self-image when our real nature is so much higher? Our real enemies are within us. They are not who we are, but we think that they are and they claim to be; that is why we find ourselves at war with ourselves. In order to discover our real identity, we have to choose sides and then fight all that is false in us until victory is won. It will be a long drawn-out battle, but the Gita's promise is that if we hold out to the end, victory is assured – precisely because this is our real nature; the rest is a masquerade.

But the very word *conflict* implies a choice. Without conflict, there is no incentive to grow; where there is a conflict, there is hope, because there are two sides. The message of the Gita is that gradually we can choose to throw more and more weight behind the pull towards our higher nature and away from the drag of separateness and conditioned behavior.

This is the choice Arjuna faces, which is why the traditional title of this first chapter of the Gita is "The Yoga of Arjuna's Despair." Even despair, as we shall see, can be a yoga – a way to wisdom – if we can see it from a higher point of view. The teaching of the Gita begins when Arjuna throws down his bow and arrows – his supports in the world he knows – and appeals to Krishna, "My will is paralyzed, and I am utterly confused. Tell me which is the better path. Let me be your disciple. I have fallen at your feet; give me instruction."

Surprisingly, given the urgency of the moment, Sri Krishna responds to this plea not with immediate help but by leading his new student step by step to that higher vantage where he can see his situation clearly and understand what it offers. His reply in chapter 2 of the Gita is a brilliant summation of the loftiest ideas in Indian philosophy – a foundation that the Gita takes for granted but is likely to be unfamiliar or misunderstood today. For that reason it will be helpful to explore that foundation first: the essential ideas of the Upanishads, which record discoveries made by sages seeking changeless truths in a world of change.

◈ *The Nature of Reality*

THE NIGHT SKY in a South Indian village is ablaze with stars, thousands more than a city-dweller can imagine. So near the equator, the march of the constellations across the sky never varies from season to season, a reassuring backdrop for the teeming activity of field and forest. Thousands of years ago a boy like me might have lain awake next to his granny watching the very same stars in the deep darkness of a tropical night, asking the same questions we ask today: What are the stars? How far away are they? What do they portend? How do I fit in?

Like ancients everywhere, my ancestors five thousand years ago studied the night sky and found patterns in it, and meaning in those patterns, driven by that age-old need to understand that is so characteristic of our species. The Gita has a good name for such people: *jijnasu,* "those with a passion to know." From their ranks come the world's great scientists and philosophers – and some of the world's greatest mystics, East and West, who share with scientists this passion to understand.

In many ways, this search for truth in ancient India followed a pattern familiar in other cultures, studying and classifying objects and creatures and seeking unities by which to explain the details – a passion for abstraction that reminds us of the ancient Greeks. But there were some – the sages who gave us India's most ancient scriptures, the Upanishads – who were not content with naming and classifying and theorizing. They wanted knowledge that was sure, invariant, something to build one's life on: a truth beyond change.

All of nature is a flux, they observed, never the same from minute to minute – not only natural phenomena but all of human experience. Whatever we cling to, wherever we look for support, will change: family, friends, country, health, social status, material welfare, everything. The mind of the observer is even less stable. Attitudes, opinions, affections shift constantly; good will gives way to ill will; trust and loyalty waver; most hurtful of all, love turns into hatred, brother against brother, friend against friend. Thought is as ever-changing as the sea. What can we depend on? Even death, so sure, is merely life's last great change: everything in our experience is in a continual process of coming into being and passing away.

Philosophers elsewhere in the ancient world made similar observations, but these seekers of the Upanishads took a different turn. Rather than reason about change, they focused on the observer: the senses, intellect, and mind. If what we know depends on what is presented to us by the senses, they asked, how reliable is this knowledge and how much can it really tell us? Can we believe that what our few senses register really embraces the whole of reality?

If human beings had no sense of hearing, they reasoned, the world we live in would be a silent one. What we call sound doesn't exist apart from what the mind makes of the waves of pressure that strike the ear. External and internal events together bring forth what we call sound. Similarly with sight: when we see a tree, objects like "leaves" with properties like "green" have no reality as such; what we see is a model that the mind has constructed to make sense of the data sent to the brain. It's a rather modern point of view, though still controversial: "All knowledge of our universe," wrote the physiologist Hudson Hoagland,

> . . . comes to us strained, if you will, through a series of highly involved physiochemical events constituting sensory reception and responses mediated by the central nervous system. We experience not the properties of objects but the properties of our own nervous systems. We can thus have no direct knowledge of reality beyond the symbols that we learn to agree upon with others who have similar nervous systems.

Consider the picture of the world that our dog Muka has.

Dogs' eyes are more limited than those of human beings, so Muka can't see all the colors that I can. I might be tempted to conclude that Muka sees only part of the world while I see it whole. But that assumes there can be only five modes of perception – that our five senses and our particular kind of nervous system are adequate for understanding the universe. I want to say my model of the world is correct and Muka's limited. Wrong, these sages reasoned: both are limited. Neither I nor Muka nor any other creature can see the world as it is, because it is unreasonable to suppose that there is no more to reality than the senses of one species on one small planet can perceive. Unless we truly believe that nothing is real except what our senses register, we must accept that there is more "out there" than what we see, hear, touch, taste, and smell.

In a critical insight, these sages brought together the world of changing phenomena outside and the world within the mind. There is no barrier between these two worlds, they realized, because the object as it is perceived cannot be separated from the act of observation. Sense and sense-object are bound together; the seer, the thing seen, and the act of seeing are aspects of a single event in consciousness. The world we live in, with its familiar forms and sensations, is a mental model whose forms have no knowable relationship with an underlying reality.

This is a subtle position, easy to misunderstand. The sages

are not saying the world we see is unreal, but simply that it is a construction of sensory data within consciousness. That construction *is* real, as real as our everyday experience. But it exists within consciousness, not "outside" – "we experience the properties of our own nervous systems" – and therefore it is inextricably bound up with change. Change in the world outside and change in the mind are the same phenomena, simply seen from different points of view. The world of experience is one undivided world of flux.

Can we then talk about an underlying reality at all? If what is real cannot be perceived by the senses or known by the mind, the search for a ground of existence underlying the phenomenal world would seem impossible.

Yet might there be a way to rise above this flux, to stand apart from this world of change within the mind? Might there be a mode of knowing higher than the mind, by which reality can be known directly? This is the question these sages asked, and its pursuit is probably India's greatest gift to the world.

Interestingly enough, another profound insight is hidden behind this question. Because the world is modeled in consciousness, they reasoned, the fact of a tremendous urge to know implies that there must be a complementary truth to be known. The passion for seeking a changeless reality is a complementary side of that very reality. It's a magnificently creative concept: when there is a rage to know, there is a reality saying, "Come and know me." That is why human beings have this passion for understanding, which the Gita would say is the force behind human growth.

The sages of the Upanishads turned Descartes' dictum inside out: "I am; therefore I think." They made the radical discovery that thinking is not a requirement for consciousness. It sounds absurd in English: isn't thinking what consciousness does? But this isn't philosophical speculation; it's an experimental observation. Instead of thinking about thinking, these sages focused attention on the thought-process itself by withdrawing attention from the senses, and when they did so, they discovered that it is possible to stand apart from the thought-process and observe it objectively.

As a result, the study of the mind in ancient India took a radically different turn from the West. In Indian thought, the study of the mind is not subjective but objective: *brahma-vidya,* "the science of reality," which has been called "the study of the mind by the mind to go beyond the mind." Its method is meditation, which in the Gita we can see presented in general terms long before it developed into different schools. I would not hesitate to call meditation one of the most important of human discoveries, an evolutionary development as important as speech or writing.

Meditation begins with withdrawing the senses from the outside world by concentrating on a focus within the mind. With the outside world forgotten, awareness becomes absorbed in the world within, a world as real and as vast as the world of the senses. In these dark depths, these sages observed and recorded all kinds of mental phenomena – how anger arises and how it can be transformed into compassion, how ill will can be changed into good will and hatred into love. As concentration deepens, thought merges in one titanic inquiry beyond words: "Who am I?" Finally, this inquiry itself dissolves and the mind becomes completely still – yet awareness remains; we are immeasurably more awake than when the mind and senses are active.

The body functions in space; the mind functions in time. In meditation, when all consciousness is retrieved from the senses into the mind, the eyes don't see, the ears don't hear; the sensory world has been left behind. In that state, if you cannot observe yourself through your senses, you – as the observer, of course, not the physical organism – don't have a body. And when awareness of the body is lost, consciousness is no longer confined in space. In practical terms, you become aware that you are not a separate creature; the sense of separateness characteristic of physical awareness has disappeared.

Similarly, when this absorption is complete, the thought-process temporarily subsides and the mind becomes still; then you are no longer in time. There are no thoughts, no sensations, only pure awareness. Beyond and beneath the world of change, there is only direct awareness of a world that is one and indivisible, infinite, radiant. Observer and observed become one in pure consciousness, pure energy, the same energy that flows through all life. And because this state is indivisible, it is not touched by time, by age, by death. It is by repeating this experience over and over again that one comes to understand and realize the words of the Gita:

> The impermanent has no reality; reality lies in the eternal. . . . You were never born; you will never die. You have never changed; you can never change. Unborn, eternal, immutable, immemorial, you do not die when the body dies. (2:16, 20)

At this depth, on the very floor of what Jung called the collective unconscious, there is no distance between "I" and "you," no distinction; we are all there together. There is no "I"; there is only all. What one experiences in that state cannot be described: with no separate observer, no distinctions or duality whatever, language breaks down; words can serve only where distinctions matter.

But that doesn't make the experience less real; in fact, it is more real than any experience in the world of duality. It can be understood, though not described, by its impact on one's life. The special, almost superhuman quality of this mode of knowing is that it enables one to live in harmony with this vision. That is its unique characteristic: not intellectual knowledge that life is indivisible, but the fact that will and heart and body and mind follow that knowledge in daily life.

Sanatana Dharma: The Key Ideas

These discoveries are the essential ideas that the Gita builds on, and since they are expressed in Sanskrit words that have no English equivalents, this is a good place to introduce the vocabulary that the Gita takes for granted.

For the direct experience of reality that comes when the mind is still, in which we see life whole, the Gita uses the same word as yoga philosophy: *samadhi.* The supreme reality itself is called Brahman; this is the divine ground of existence, the bedrock of reality, the indivisible unity in which all creation is one.

Since this unity is absolute, beyond all change, Brahman has no attributes, so it cannot be described. Yet its discovery brings experiential awareness of an inner presence far greater than the individual personality, from which the body draws its strength, the senses draw their activity, the intellect draws its powers, and the heart draws its capacity to love. This presence is called simply Atman, "Self."

Like Brahman, the Atman is pure consciousness. When the mind is still, it has no limitations to distinguish it from the rest of the field of consciousness – "like pure water poured into pure water," as the Upanishads say. The ineffable core of pure consciousness within each creature is exactly the same as the core of pure consciousness in every other creature; there is no difference at all. In the Upanishads this is put into an equation as precise and profound as Einstein's formula for the equivalence of mass and energy: *Tat tvam asi,* "You are That": your real Self is identical with that ultimate reality beyond name and form.

Brahman has a passive aspect – attributeless reality – and a dynamic aspect which is pure energy, called *prakriti.* Prakriti is both primordial energy and the material world manifested from it – that is, the whole phenomenal world, Brahman as seen through the filter of the mind in motion. In remarkably modern language, the Gita refers to prakriti – mind, matter, and energy all together – as a field:

> I am the Knower of the field in everyone, Arjuna.
> Knowledge of the field and its Knower is true knowl-
> edge. (13:2)

These are tremendous ideas, radically different from the traditional view that mind and matter, God and creation, are separate and distinct. In traditional language, the Gita is saying that the ultimate reality most religions call God is not separate from the world. It is not inaccurate to say that the world is created by God, but the Gita and Upanishads would say also that the world emanates from God, and even that the world *is* God – not in the pantheistic sense, but in the sense that when we look at reality through duality, the world is what we see.

I want to stress that these are experiential discoveries, made not only in ancient India but again and again, independently, in other cultures and times. For that reason Western philosophers began calling these ideas *philosophia perennis,* "the perennial philosophy," but that suggests speculation rather than experience. The Gita is not presenting theology or metaphysics but sanatana dharma: the "eternal law," the fundamental unity of life.

Because we are not separate from this supreme reality, it follows that each of us is incomplete so long as we consider ourselves separate: that is, until we make this discovery ourselves. Whatever else we may achieve in life, whether we become billionaires or win the Nobel Prize or marry the superstar of our dreams, there will be a vacuum in our hearts that can be filled only by direct, experiential knowledge of reality. This is the message of the Gita in a nutshell: life has only one purpose, and that is to know the divine ground of existence and become united with it here and now.

So sanatana dharma, the perennial philosophy, can be summarized in three simple propositions:

First, at the basis of consciousness, in the very depths of the heart, there is a living, undying spirit that in Sanskrit is called Atman, the Self, which is present in every creature.

Second, in all the great religions there has come down a body of disciplines by which we can discover this divine spirit ourselves, not after death but here on earth.

And third, making this discovery – realizing the Atman or "Self-realization," using the word *realize* in its root sense of making something real in one's own experience – is the supreme purpose of life, the purpose for which we were born.

Levels of Reality

One all-important idea here is that the way in which reality is seen and described varies according to the level of consciousness of the observer. In other words, there are levels of reality, corresponding to the level of observation.

This is an elusive idea, but one that is vitally important for understanding the Bhagavad Gita, which will present us with the same one reality in a confusing variety of ways. The explanation of this is that since awareness is shaped by the mind of the observer, the ultimate reality takes the form that answers one's deepest needs. Culture and tradition come into this, of course, but it is essentially a matter of the observer's own consciousness. Thus, says the Rig Veda, though God is one, we call him – or her, or it – by different names.

India has always embraced diversity, so we find there many names and faces for the one divine reality – Shiva, Vishnu, and the Divine Mother, among others, each endowed with attributes that a human being can relate to and love and worship. Vishnu, "the all-pervasive," himself has further forms, including Krishna. Then there are the *devas*, "gods" in lowercase – personifications of the forces of nature perhaps absorbed into Indian religion from an earlier age and preserved as divine powers. The panoply is confusing to almost everyone not born in India, to whom it often appears that Hindus worship different gods. Indians themselves add to this confusion by speaking affectionately of "the gods" meaning any of the above; but if pressed, even an illiterate villager knows that these are only faces or personalities of the same divine reality, like a repertory actor playing several roles.

I can give a personal illustration of this. My ancestral family has worshipped God as Shiva for centuries, and my devout grandmother was no exception. At the time of her death, however, her vision of God was of Rama, another incarnation of Vishnu. But her daughter, my mother, reverted to Shiva; and I, who grew up without any particular devotion, have become a kind of divine defector to Sri Krishna. All this within a matriarchal tradition in a region of India where God has been worshipped as the Divine Mother since time immemorial.

Indian thought takes this one step further: in response to the collective needs of many, the needs of the times, God takes form – is incarnated – as a human being. Sri Krishna explains in famous lines:

My true being is unborn and changeless. I am the Lord who dwells in every creature. Through the power of my own maya, I manifest myself in a finite form. Whenever dharma declines and the purpose of life is forgotten, I manifest myself on earth. I am born in every age to protect the good, to destroy evil, and to reestablish dharma. . . . As people approach me, so I receive them. All paths, Arjuna, lead to me. (4:6–8, 11)

In the Bhagavad Gita, we encounter Sri Krishna in virtually all these aspects: as the divine incarnation who is Arjuna's friend and guide and charioteer; as a form or aspect of God as Vishnu, the sustainer of the universe; and as the impersonal divine essence in all things:

> But beyond prakriti I have another, higher nature, Arjuna, which supports the whole universe and is the source of life in all beings. In these two aspects of my nature is the womb of all creation. The birth and dissolution of the cosmos itself take place in me. . . .
>
> I am the taste of pure water, Arjuna, and the radiance of the sun and moon. I am the sacred word and the sound heard in air, and the courage of human beings. I am the sweet fragrance in the earth and the radiance of fire; I am the life in every creature and the striving of the spiritual aspirant. (7:5–6, 8–9)

> I am the true Self in the heart of every creature, Arjuna, and the beginning, middle, and end of their existence.
> . . . I am death, which overcomes all, and the source of all beings still to be born. . . . I am the gambling of the gambler and the radiance in all that shines. I am effort, I am victory, and I am the goodness of the virtuous. . . . Wherever you find strength or beauty or spiritual

power, you may be sure that these have sprung from a spark of my essence. (10:20–41 *passim*)

But this cosmic form – God as all that is – is not an abstraction to be expressed in poetry. It confers a terrifying vision, for it embraces the entire universe in its eternal cycle of creation and destruction. This is the vision Arjuna begs for and receives in chapter 11 of the Gita, despite Sri Krishna's warning that it is more than human sight can bear, more dazzling than a thousand suns, and he is utterly overwhelmed:

ARJUNA:

O Lord, I see within your body all the gods and every kind of living creature. . . . I see you everywhere, without beginning, middle, or end. You are the Lord of all creation, and the cosmos is your body. As rivers flow into the ocean, all the warriors of this world are passing into your fiery jaws; all creatures rush to their destruction like moths into a flame. You lap the worlds into your burning mouths and swallow them. Filled with your terrible radiance, O Vishnu, the whole of creation bursts into flames. Tell me who you are, O Lord of terrible form. I bow before you; have mercy! I want to know who you are, you who existed before all creation. Your nature and workings confound me.

SRI KRISHNA:

I am time, the destroyer of all; I have come to consume
the world. (11:15–32 *passim*)

The supreme reality is all these things, and more and none;
it is both formless and has forms, and yet is beyond both; it
cannot be limited in any way. It is our human understanding
– the state of consciousness with which reality is viewed – that
gives apparent form to what is formless. In the passages just
quoted, Sri Krishna does not change; Arjuna sees him differently in different states of awareness. Changing the level of
consciousness changes the way we see: it is as simple as that,
yet on this simple observation hinge virtually all the insights
of the Gita into how to live.

In the Gita's view, then, the world has really two layers –
two levels of reality. The first level is what we see around us –
the green hills I enjoy on a drive to San Francisco, the Golden
Gate, the Bay sparkling with sunlight and flecked with sail-
boats: what philosophers call the phenomenal world, the
world of change. This is the surface layer of reality, the skin,
so to say. It seems real, but on close inspection, as we have
seen, appearances resolve into transitory sense-data with
only the relative reality of a dream. Yet underlying this is a
deeper level that is invisible, beyond time and change, beyond
the senses yet supporting what they present to us, from which

they draw their reality: the noumenal layer, the "world within the world."

This gives us a criterion for reality: only that is ultimately real which never changes. Anything that goes on changing is never the same, so it cannot be real; to be real, it should be constant always.

It is in this respect that the Gita says the world is not ultimately real. Its reality is relative to the observer – not to the neurological apparatus of a particular individual but to the Self, the Atman. The faculty of knowing belongs not to the faculties of perception but to the Self, "the Knower of the field." It's a crude analogy, but if we think of the individual as a light bulb, the intelligence of the Self is like electricity: there may be many bulbs, but all draw on the same current.

Conditioned as we are to look upon the external world alone as real, this is difficult to grasp. But in the Gita's view, it means that everything – you, me, the world around us, the cosmos with its billions of galaxies – draws its reality from the Self. Without this transcendent observer, the phenomenal world doesn't exist.

This difficult statement has highly practical consequences. "We see as we are": when we look at the world through the senses and intellect, we see discrete objects and separate individuals; when we view the world as the Atman – beyond duality – we see life whole. On the physical level, when I look at you, I don't see you; I see your body. But when the mind is still, I see you as you are: as the Self, who is one and the same in all. So the Gita says:

> Whatever exists, Arjuna, animate or inanimate, is born through the union of the field and its Knower. They alone see truly who see the Lord the same in every creature, who see the Deathless in the hearts of all that die. (13:26–27)

These levels give a glimpse of our potential as human beings. We can actually move upward – or down – on this scale of reality; we become more real as we move closer to the Atman, our real Self. Life on the surface – living for the moment, living only for ourselves – is unreal because we are constantly changing, pushed and pulled in different directions by our disparate desires. Such lives may as well be written on water, with as little choice as in a dream. So far as the Gita is concerned, this is the ultimate in unreality. But when, through meditation, we change to a higher level of consciousness and see the same Self in all, we move towards the other end of the scale of reality, marked by men and women like Mahatma Gandhi or Thérèse of Lisieux whose lives endure long after their bodies have fallen away. It is, Sri Krishna says, the difference between night and day:

Such a sage awakes to light in the night of all creatures.

That which the world calls day is the night of ignorance
to the wise. (2:69)

A Compassionate Universe

In a beautiful verse, speaking now as a divine
incarnation, Sri Krishna tells Arjuna simply, "There is nothing beyond me." The entire universe is only one of the manifestations of God. Even if astronomers discover billions of
clusters of galaxies beyond the billions already known, they
would all be within the realm of Brahman:

There is nothing that exists separate from me, Arjuna.
The entire universe is suspended from me as my necklace of jewels. (7:7)

What then is our place here, tucked away on a small planet
orbiting a second-rate sun on the edge of one galaxy among
billions?

On the physical level, of course, the answer is familiar:
we're not much to write home about. But if we take the Gita's
view, that God has become the world and mind and matter
belong to the same field, we get a much loftier view of evolution: the eons-long rise of consciousness from pure energy
until the simplest of life-forms emerges and the struggle for
increasing self-awareness begins. In the Gita's view, we can
look on life as a play with the world as a stage for learning

who we are – moving closer and closer to reality until we realize our identity with the Self. To put it dramatically, the whole cosmos is a setting for us to rise above it and go beyond time, place, and circumstance into the supreme reality that is God.

Now we are going to the heart of Indian mysticism: this is all a play. We are dressed up with paint on our faces, paint on our minds, and we go about believing we are separate individuals. As long as we are in this play, we are caught up in the performance – like, say, Sir Laurence Olivier playing a role. But in the supreme climax of Self-realization we discover that we are really the Self just playing a part. Then it is that we can play our roles beautifully: as father or mother, as daughter or son, as friend or helpmate, no longer identifying with the character of the moment that struts and frets upon the stage but sure in the knowledge that when the curtain is rung down, we can take our bows and go home.

That is what the Gita is trying to convey. We are not petty, separate creatures subject to birth and death; we are sparks from the divine fire from which the universe came billions of years ago. And it's like the theater: we are necessary for this play. Without actors and actresses and the audience, there wouldn't be any theater at all.

We shouldn't press this image too closely. Life as we know it, with its joys and tragedies, is terribly real. But we are here to learn, and that includes to help. In any situation we can learn to grow, passing from lower levels of reality to the highest. Each of us, the Gita says, contains all of life; in each, as consciousness, is contained the entire universe. The proof comes when we see everyone in ourselves and ourselves in all, which is the basis of universal love:

> They alone see truly who see the Lord the same in every
> creature, who see the Deathless in the hearts of all that
> die. (13:27)

This brings the vast cosmology of the Gita back home and down to earth. After all, in a personal sense, we – the observer – *are* the center of the universe as we experience it. Far from leaving the human being isolated in a pointless existence in a far corner of a lackluster galaxy, we live at home in a compassionate universe that is part of us, with the capacity to live in a way that benefits the rest of life.

◇ *The End of Sorrow*

THIS IS AN inspiring vision, but when we reflect on it, doubts may creep in. Do I really want this "universal Self" if it means losing my personality?

Perhaps Arjuna had similar questions, because right after this glorious summary of sanatana dharma and Self-realization, he asks on behalf of all of us, "Well, but what's it really like?"

> Tell me of those who live established in wisdom, ever
> aware of the Self, O Krishna. How do they talk? How
> sit? How move about? (2:54)

Arjuna is a practical man – a warrior, after all, a man of action, not a philosopher. He is asking, "How can I recognize those who have realized the unity of life? What are their distinguishing characteristics? I don't want to hear philosophy or metaphysics; I want to know how they live. If things don't go their way, do they get angry? When challenges come, do they run away? When they're annoyed, do they take it out on those around them? Do they show grace under pressure, or do they get upset and say, 'Don't come near me, I've had a bad day'?"

Arjuna doesn't use words like *God* or *superconscious*. He asks about being *sthitaprajna* – "established in prajna," the highest wisdom, so firmly established that even if the whole world tries to blow him off his feet, it cannot. We ordinary human beings are just the opposite, pulled this way and that by urges and cravings; the moment something beckons, we run after it. To live intentionally, we need to establish sovereignty over every level of consciousness, which is what this word *sthitaprajna* implies.

Krishna's answers paint the portrait of an illumined man or woman as deftly as Leonardo. He begins with one telling phrase: "Such a person has done away with all selfish desires." That's the whole answer in a nutshell.

But it's scarcely an inviting way to start. We can almost hear Arjuna thinking, "All? Can't I keep just a few – one, five, you can count them on one hand. I have hundreds of them; I'll give up all but five." Sri Krishna says, "All. Every selfish desire must go."

Then, seeing Arjuna's expression, he explains: There are no selfish desires in this state because there's nothing to desire; you have it all. You are completely satisfied, in the Self by the Self alone. And he expands on the practical consequences:

They live in wisdom who see themselves in all and all in
them, who have renounced every selfish desire and
sense craving tormenting the heart.

Neither agitated by grief nor hankering after pleasure,
they live free from lust and fear and anger. Established in
meditation, they are truly wise. Fettered no more by selfish attachments, they are neither elated by good fortune
nor depressed by bad. Such are the seers. . . .

As rivers flow into the ocean but cannot make the
vast ocean overflow, so flow the streams of the sense-
world into the sea of peace that is the sage. But this is
not so with the desirer of desires.

They are forever free who renounce all selfish desires
and break out of the ego-cage of *I* and *mine* to be united
with the Lord. This is the supreme state. Attain to this,
and pass from death to immortality. (2:55–57, 70–72)

Freedom is the watchword here, as it is throughout the Gita.
It means that no emotion can overwhelm you, no craving
can drive you into action. As long as you have self-centered
desires, Sri Krishna is saying, you are dependent upon others,
dependent upon outside circumstances, the plaything of fortune. Unless you find your center of gravity within yourself,
you cannot help manipulating people to bring about your fulfillment – a compulsion that can wreck any relationship, as

most of us know to our cost. Once you realize your identity with the Self, however, you are your own support. You need nothing, and nothing can shake you. Your heart is full, and when your heart is full of joy and your mind full of peace, where is the need to manipulate anyone? You are always complete, whatever others give, whatever life takes away.

One of the first fruits of this freedom is that depression can no longer touch you. Rough winds will blow, but nothing can make you feel unequal to what life sends. It is not that you won't face difficult situations, but there will be no agitation in your mind, which means you won't lose your nerve. You will be able to work continuously without burning out or losing concentration. Things can go wrong, people can attack you; it won't affect your capacity to work – and every day will be new for you; every day will be fresh.

In this state, to borrow an image from St. Teresa of Avila, all the bees of desire that are wandering about – in the shopping center, the theater, the casino, the clubs, the beach – come back to the hive of the heart. That is where the honey is being made. When absorption in this state of consciousness is complete, the mind is flooded with an almost unbearable joy, one taste of which makes the pleasures of the senses pale. No words or thoughts can describe the supreme felicity of this state. How can you describe the indescribable? How can you capture in words a state from which words and thoughts turn back frightened?

All this sets personality ablaze. Years ago, when I began teaching meditation in the U.S., I was asked if Self-realization means becoming a zombie. I had to explain that in the Gita's view, life as most of us live it is embarrassingly automatic. Far from having fascinating personalities, each of us goes about wearing the same mask with minor variations and responding to life with the same basic urges and fears. Only when these masks are removed does personality begin to shine. If you want to see true originals, look at men and women like Mahatma Gandhi, Teresa of Avila, Jalaluddin Rumi, Francis of Assisi, each of them one of a kind. In my experience, Gandhi's personality was like a noose; if you went near him, he could snare you in love and remove all fear from your heart.

The Unitive Vision

Most important, instead of separateness, in this state you see life whole. The world doesn't change; your mode of seeing has changed – your capacity to see, your capacity to understand. You see beneath appearances while enjoying the diversity in appearance. Then every little thing glows with the grace of God. That is where the joy comes: a continuing awareness that never leaves you even for a moment.

It is important to remember here that Arjuna asked about being "*established* in wisdom": not just having the experience of unity, but living in it at every moment. In Sanskrit this is called *sahaja samadhi* – samadhi that is with you always. At first you see the Self only in deep meditation; after that experience you return to ordinary awareness. You know beyond doubt that the separateness you see is an illusion, but you still *see* separateness. The experience of unity must be repeated over and over and over again for the direct awareness of unity to become continuous. Then you live in samadhi even with your eyes open, acting creatively in all the normal challenges of life without any disturbance in the unitive state.

It requires great skill and artistry to learn to do this in the midst of a normal, active life – and not a little motivation too, for the joy of this experience brings with it a great temptation to bask in it rather than return to the trials and sorrows of daily life. But for those with an overriding desire to be of service in the world, it is possible to learn to keep one eye on unity and the other on multiplicity, one eye on the eternal Self and the other on life's passing show. Without this skill, you cannot relate to people lovingly or work effectively in the service of others – and if I may say so, others cannot relate easily to you as well.

Once established in this state, however, you see the world as Spinoza described it, the finite resting upon the infinite. You see the finite with your physical senses, but you are always aware that what gives support to each apparently separate thing and creature is the Self, from which all creation comes.

This image of Spinoza's always reminds me of the sea,

ceaselessly in motion on the surface with miles of deep water below. When I saw the ocean for the first time, it was essentially just a large body of water; I don't think it had any other connotation. Later, when I became intoxicated with English poetry, lines like those from Lord Byron – "Roll on, thou deep and dark blue Ocean – roll! Ten thousand fleets sweep over thee in vain" – added another dimension. The sea was no longer just a body of water; it acquired associations, history, majesty, sonority. But by the time I began teaching meditation, I was so absorbed in the Gita that I saw the ocean as Sri Krishna describes it, a manifestation of the power of God:

All right, Arjuna, I will tell you of my divine powers. I will mention only the most glorious, for there is no end to them.

I am the true Self in the heart of every creature, Arjuna, and the beginning, middle, and end of their existence. Among the shining gods I am Vishnu; of luminaries I am the sun; among the storm gods I am Marichi, and in the night sky I am the moon.

Among scriptures I am the Sama Veda, and among the lesser gods I am Indra. Among the senses I am the mind, and in living beings I am consciousness. . . . Among bodies of water I am the ocean . . . and among mountains I am the Himalayas. (10:19–22, 24–25)

This is not just poetry. How we see the world determines

how we relate to it. When you see God everywhere, you treat everything with respect for the divinity that shines through it. Oil spills are not just tragic; they are desecration. Dumping trash and sewage and pollutants into the ocean is desecration. Seeing that God has become the world brings not just respect but reverence for every thing and creature in it.

In this vision you still see the splendor of the universe, but not with your physical eyes. We see not so much with the eyes as with consciousness, so when the illusion of separateness is lifted, "we behold what we are, and we are what we behold": unbroken awareness of God, whose face is everywhere. Beyond space and time, you are right back with the big bang, right on the front seat. You see how life comes, evolving from unity into multiplicity, all things and creatures as forms of the one supreme reality.

In a sense, the world you see is the same; yet it is no longer the same; it is transformed. Formerly the phenomenal world had a partial reality; now it shares in the supreme reality. Formerly you saw the world; now you see into the world – see the core of the divine spirit, if you like, that throbs at the very heart of life as the Atman in every creature. In the language of philosophy, you see the world both as God immanent and as Brahman, God transcendent.

The observer too is absorbed in this vision. Just as the waters of a river cease to belong to that river when joining the sea, you lose the illusion of separate identity when you merge in the sea of this unitive reality. The individual human being is not lost but multiplied infinitely; you see your connections with every creature.

This is not just the beauty that the poet or the artist or the scientist sees. It is a total identification with the whole of the universe in which sea and sky, mountains and rivers, all come together as one – an inner radiance that speaks to you directly as the reflection of the glory of God. It is not a reaction to the sheer intoxicating appeal of the senses, however beautiful that may be; it is not a reaction at all but a union. I think this sense of being united with the mountains and forests and the ocean and the starry night is behind the rapture that poets sometimes glimpse in moments of mystical insight. Yet as much as I admire literature and the works of art and science, the realization of the unity of life cannot be conveyed through any other art than the supreme art of living – by returning good will for ill will, friendship for enmity, compassion for anger, love for hatred.

The End of Sorrow

One of the most appealing fruits of this experience is that you become a stranger to loneliness – an utter stranger. All separateness is gone. You don't have to close your eyes to see God; what else is there to see? You see the divinity in every creature, so your love goes out to all. Anger subsides and becomes love, fear subsides and becomes courage, greed subsides and becomes compassion. Without a sense of "I" and "mine," you live in all and everyone lives in you. Even when you are alone, you are at one with the world. It's not a social enjoyment; it's a kind of enlightened rapture of watching yourself in many disguises – not as other people, but as yourself playing various roles. That is how the joy comes.

And this brings an end to sorrow. I have seen children in India start crying as soon as they see their mother, then stop when they're in her arms. When the mother asks, "Why were you crying?" the little one replies, "I don't remember." That's what happens when the illusion of a separate self disappears: you forget to cry for yourself, because the very source of personal sorrow falls away.

This is difficult to explain, but terribly important because it is so often misunderstood. Everybody has times when misfortune strikes us or those we love. Everybody grieves at such times; each of us takes these crises personally. When your sense of separateness vanishes, you experience such tragedies for everyone – and with such a vast field to absorb your capacity for sorrow, there is very little left for dwelling on your own suffering. Those who suffer most in life are those who dwell upon themselves so extensively that they can't think about others. Conversely, those who suffer least are those who do not dwell upon themselves. It is the separate ego that feels personal suffering, and that separate self is rather like a dream – not unreal, but barely remembered in waking life. In dreams we are happy, we are sad, but when we wake up, the dream world melts away. We know that in reality there was no pleasure and no sorrow. In the dream, we believed that there was pain; therefore we felt pain. Similarly, when your ego is hurt, it suffers, and because you identify yourself with your ego, you suffer. When you don't identify yourself with your ego, sorrow goes out of your life.

We want to protest, "Don't you feel any grief, then?" Of course you do. You haven't become insensitive; your sensitivity has simply been absorbed in the needs of everyone, joys and sorrows alike. It brings a joy and security that no power on earth can shake. When you go to the dentist, your body may suffer: the body is physical; it obeys physical laws. But in your heart is abiding peace, a joy that will never leave you. Of course you grieve! When half a billion people go to bed hungry, you don't have to see them; they are in your consciousness all the time. But there is nothing that can cause you grief personally because you don't put any demands on life for yourself. You don't try to clutch at people for support; you don't cling to pleasure or depend upon appreciation; you are satisfied in and by your Self alone. "Having attained that abiding joy," the Gita says, "there is no more to desire. You cannot be shaken even by the heaviest burden of sorrow." (6:21–22)

In this state, though inwardly your mind is still, outwardly you may be ceaselessly active in selfless service. Full inside, you don't need anything, but you are restless to give, to serve.

This union of contemplation and action is a hallmark of the Gita, which urges us not to withdraw from the world but to conquer all selfishness and then throw ourselves into selfless service right in the midst of life, where there is so much pain, so much sorrow, so much violence, that every day there are things to be done:

> It is not those who lack energy or refrain from action,
> but those who work without expectation of reward
> who attain the goal of meditation. (6:1)

> Selfish action imprisons the world. Act selflessly, with-
> out any thought of personal profit. . . . Every selfless act,
> Arjuna, is born from Brahman, the eternal, infinite
> Godhead; he is present in every act of service. . . .
> Therefore, strive constantly to serve the welfare of the
> world. . . . Do your work with the welfare of others
> always in mind. (3:9, 15, 19–20)

This is what the Gita calls "action in inaction": stillness at the center, but immense energy released for the service of all:

> The wise see that there is action in the midst of inaction
> and inaction in the midst of action. Their conscious-
> ness is unified, and every act is done with complete
> awareness. (4:18)

CHAPTER FOUR

◈ *Levels of Personality*

KRISHNA HAS GIVEN a lofty glimpse of what it means to reach our full human potential, but there is a great deal hiding our real Self – covering it up, if you like, in dense layers of mistaken identity.

Here again there are levels of reality. Most of us, when asked who we are, answer in physical terms: "I'm an engineer, five foot seven, black hair, live in California." But of course that is only part of the answer: we are describing the body, where it is, what it does. There is an inner self – or selves! – as well.

I came across a perfect illustration of these levels of personality when a friend showed me a Russian doll shaped like an egg, apparently made from one piece of wood. I had never seen a doll like this, so I turned it around in my hands admiring its artistry. Then, anticipating my surprise, my friend took the doll back, held it up before my eyes, and twisted it open. What had seemed solid was only a shell; inside was another doll exactly like it but smaller, fitted to the outer one as nicely as a hand inside a glove. This is the Gita's idea of body and mind: one hidden inside the other and possessing the same form, because there is a direct correspondence between the two.

Teresa of Avila has a nice turn on this image: she invites us to think of ourselves as a castle with concentric chambers made of pure crystal. Imagine a Russian doll made of crystal; wouldn't it be beautiful? In the Gita's version, the outermost shell, the body, would be opaque, but the one inside would be a bit translucent. And at the very center would be the Atman, which shines as pure intelligence. The mind, being closer to the light of the Atman, reveals some of that light; the body, material and furthest from the Atman, reveals very little. In a highly creative person – a scientist like Einstein, a poet like Milton, an artist like Michelangelo – some of this light does shine through. The more we identify with the Self, the Gita would say, the brighter our whole life will be. Conversely, if we think we are no more than the body, very little of what Browning calls the "imprisoned splendor" within us can shine forth.

In fact, this idea that we are the body is the most monstrous superstition that humanity is subject to. No case of mistaken identity could cause greater grief. At the very least, as William James put it, this is so limiting a view that it leads us to think and act as if we had no more resources than our little finger.

When we talk about superstitions, we think of things like

seeing a black cat on the day of finals means a C minus. Superstitions like that are harmless, but the belief that we are the body is disastrous because we base our lives on it. As a result, every attitude of ours is likely to be wrong.

When I learned in elementary school that the earth is really round, I raced home to tell my mother and grandmother the news. Granny didn't say anything. It didn't matter to her if the earth were cubical or shaped like a doughnut; one could always lead a selfless life. But when I told my mother that the earth is round, she was stunned.

"That's right," I said. "This is what they have discovered in the West. We just learned it at school."

She just laughed. "This is what we send you to school for? Look out the kitchen window. Go to Palghat and ask; talk to people in Madras. Everybody knows the earth is flat."

Similarly, almost everyone today will tell you there is nothing beyond the physical body. Yet the world within is every bit as real – and neither of these is who we really are. Body and mind are both fields of action for our real Self, the Atman, living in the house of the body and sleeping in the bedroom of the mind.

I don't think there has been any time during the last few centuries when the image of the human being has been so obsessively physical. Everywhere we go, we find this superstition repeated, and each exposure conditions us a bit more. On the one hand, the brilliant progress in the neurosciences seems to have reduced the mind to electrical epiphenomena of the brain, while in popular culture the emphasis on physical appearance couldn't be more obsessive. In one recent magazine, for example, I saw a lush advertisement maintaining that my real self is blonde; another advised me I could project a more appealing personality with a different cut of jacket. When we go on seeing this kind of thing over and over again in the media, hearing it over and over in popular songs, it sinks into deeper consciousness until finally there is no intellectual way of getting it out. We can read all the books in the university library, watch any number of self-improvement shows on TV; we will still be in the same confusion.

This root superstition breeds other superstitions. Once we believe we are the body, a host of similar assumptions follows. "If I fill this body with things to eat, I'll be satisfied. If I deck this body with clothes and jewelry, I'll be beautiful. If I fill each day with pleasures and excitement, I'll be happy." And so on, ignoring the fact that the needs of the mind can't possibly be filled by the body, and that beauty comes from within.

One of the problems with seeking satisfaction in physical ways is that the more we try, the less we get. There *is* pleasure for a limited period; nobody denies that. But sensations are short-lived, and it is the nature of the physical body to get surfeited. Physical sensations are like eating a meal; after a while the body has had enough. But the desire for satisfaction remains, so the mind goes on seeking, and the longer it tries, the less satisfaction we get and the more frustrated we become. That is why the Gita keeps repeating that there is no satisfaction in anything finite. Our need is not for five minutes of pleasure, nor even five hundred years; our need is for something that lasts forever.

Believing we are the body means we are going to commit a lot of mistakes – likely to do all sorts of absurd things to satisfy emotional or spiritual needs in physical ways that only make us more body-conscious, making the problem worse.

To begin with, identifying with something that is constantly changing is a perfect recipe for insecurity. Everyone wants to keep the body healthy and attractive, but when we start thinking that is who we are, we are fighting a battle with change that no human being has ever won, constantly losing ground in the inevitable decline from those golden years around age eighteen.

Second, as long as we believe we are the body, we can't help believing that everyone else is a body too, each separate from us and from each other. Then it seems natural, even right, to treat our personal interests as separate from theirs, even if getting what we want comes at their expense.

Third, when we identify ourselves with the body, we cannot help believing that we can change ourselves by changing the way we look. So much time and attention goes into playing games with physical appearances! It's like spending our lives fixing up a house we never get around to living in. We design it, build it, plaster it, paint it, furnish it, decorate it and redecorate it over and over, but before we take up residence, we go into the grave.

I read all sorts of hair-raising things in popular magazines about how we can enrich our personality this way. If I wear a turtleneck, I have the "now look"; if I have an open collar, I suppose I have the "then look" – until tomorrow, when turtlenecks are "then" again and some other neck is in. We are so conditioned by this kind of talk that we believe clothes adorn us. The Gita would say no, it is we who adorn our clothes, because the only real beauty comes from within.

Recently, while Christine was shopping in a big department store, I found a seat at the cosmetics counter. I learned a great deal just sitting there, the gist of which was that by putting various kinds of stuff around my eyes and adding "handcrafted eyelashes," I could get a new look and become a new me.

Near my chair was a little workshop where a specialist was teaching customers how to smile. To me it looked frightful: you bare four teeth, you know, two above and two below, and hold it for the appropriate time: fifty seconds for an acquaintance, sixty seconds for a friend, ninety seconds for someone you really like. I've seen people who have been trained to smile like this; it just doesn't work. Nothing can make a smile come from the heart. When someone greets you with a smile and says, "I've waited so long to meet you," just look at the eyes. The lips may be showing the right number of teeth, but the eyes are saying, "If I never see you again, it will be too soon."

The main problem with identifying ourselves with the body is that we spend our lives trying to satisfy nonphysical needs in physical ways. It is as if there is a hole in our consciousness that has no bottom, and day after day we pour into this fathomless pit all the things we think will fill it: bank checks, stock certificates, material possessions, tokens of power and prestige, every fleeting satisfaction of the day. We find a little pleasure or profit and toss it in; we never even hear it hit the bottom, so we try again. This goes on and on and on; we just don't know what else to try. Sri Krishna would object, "This is a *bottomless* hole. How can you fill it up? That which is infinite can be filled only with something infinite." The deepest driving need in our consciousness is not for any finite pleasure or object or experience, but for something without limits: the direct, personal, experiential knowledge of the eternal reality that is within.

This problem becomes most acute when we try to fill this need through romantic relationships, where we are most vulnerable. Then we are staking our happiness on something outside ourselves – someone we really have no control over, and who is probably staking their happiness on us at the same time, with equal likelihood of success. Most of us have gone through this kind of relationship at one time or another.

Once the period of pleasure is over, the period of frustration begins. We may know intellectually that it's not good for us to associate with that person, it's not good to go about with that person, it's not good to long for that person, but whatever we do, when the clock strikes seven we'll be standing on her doorstep hoping to take her out, waiting at home for him to call. Then, if what we long for actually happens, we find ourselves saying afterwards, "Why did I have to bring this on myself again?" And if nothing happens that night, we become even more frustrated and want it all the more. As long as we look for happiness outside ourselves, the Gita would say, life can hold us hostage – and, tragically, it often strikes through those we love.

In Sanskrit, this mistaken identification with the body is called *avidya,* which simply means ignorance: mistaking the perishable for the permanent, the finite for the infinite, the separate for the whole. This is ignorance on a truly colossal scale. It's a good term. No judgment is implied, no wickedness, no stupidity; we simply have something to learn – not intellectually, but through personal experience.

An Inner Body

In the Gita, both body and mind are considered tools of consciousness: the body is an external instrument and the mind an internal instrument. We are neither; we are the Self, the operator, who uses body and mind as powerful tools for mastering the art of living. We can think of these two together as the car we drive; the body is the chassis and the mind the engine.

Indian philosophy goes so far as to call both of these two "bodies," which is one reason Russian dolls make such an apt illustration. Just as we have a physical body, according to this idea, we have a mental or "subtle" body consisting of thoughts, memories, desires, and other such intangibles. The physical body, being physical, is subject to decay; but the subtle body is a field of forces, which are nonphysical in the sense that they are not measurable in the objective world. But that doesn't make them less real. We can't see electricity, but we can see the effects of it. Similarly, though we can't see anger, we can see the effects of it, not only in damaged relationships but even in damage to the body in heart attack or stroke. And although we can't see forgiveness, we can see the effects of it in the healing of emotional wounds.

James Clerk Maxwell found that electricity and magnetism, which seem so different in everyday life, are different expressions of a single force. Similarly, sankhya traces the thousand and one emotions we experience during the day to a handful of deeper forces called *samskaras* in Sanskrit, which express themselves differently under different conditions.

The most virulent of these in the Gita are the Big Three: selfish desire, anger, and fear. These three are closely related, but each has its own tactics. Selfish desire – *kama,* often translated as lust – is the fever of sensory craving. Anger – *krodha,* which covers a gamut from background resentments to out-right rage – is essentially an expression of self-will, the violent drive to have one's own way. And fear – *bhaya,* which includes vague emotions like anxiety and insecurity – arises from separateness: feeling isolated and alone in an alien world. In fact, as you can see, all three flow from this acute sense of sep-arateness from the whole; and therefore the root of all these is the sense of a separate self, which is both the source and the result of body-consciousness.

The subtle body, therefore, is not a thing but a process. This is a key point, because a process can be changed – redirected, transformed, even stilled, if one only knows how.

Like electricity and magnetism, the forces in the mind shape the field around them – the field called prakriti, the uni-versal ground of the phenomenal world. In this field, every action leaves an impression; and since this includes all action, mental as well as physical, even thoughts have consequences that affect the field, leaving impressions that act on each other and build up with repetition – accumulated effects that last much, much longer than their material causes.

The personal implications of this are staggering: the subtle body contains the record of all our thoughts. Every thought we think is registered in this inner body! And since thoughts record our experiences and are themselves expressed in words and actions, the subtle body may be said to contain the accumulated record of our lives.

In the 1930s, a brilliant Canadian neurosurgeon named Wilder Penfield happened by accident upon a similar kind of record in the brain. Since the brain itself does not feel pain, Dr. Penfield had developed a way of using only local anesthesia during surgery so that he could talk with the patient while probing areas of the brain with mild current from an electrode. In the midst of one such operation, one of his patients suddenly began to describe a scene she recognized from her past, which she was experiencing again in full detail. As long as the probe remained at that particular location in her brain, the experience continued; when the probe was removed, the experience ceased – but later, whenever that part of the brain was stimulated, the same experience would be replayed, as vividly as before.

After this startling discovery, Penfield observed the same phenomenon in other patients. Each insisted that the experience was not like a memory or a vivid dream, but exactly like living through the event again. Penfield came to the conclusion that the nervous system contains a detailed library of past experiences locked into specific locations in the human brain.

This is not the same as the library of impressions in the subtle body; the brain seems too plastic for every memory to be enshrined forever in a particular physical location. But Dr.

Penfield's observations provide a dramatic illustration of how much more of the past our consciousness contains than we might guess – a critical point when we look later at what the Gita says happens at the time of death.

Even More "Selves" . . .

Of course, if you have seen real Russian dolls, you know that one inside the other is not the end of the story. That second doll can be opened to reveal another, and so on, each tinier than the one before.

Similarly, in the Gita, this inner doll we have been calling the subtle body is really not just one. In this view, what we call mind has really three components. Nearest to the body is the field of personal thoughts and emotions, which we can agree to go on calling the mind. But there is also what is sometimes called the "higher mind" – in Sanskrit, *buddhi,* a word with no English equivalent; it comprises will, judgment, discernment, and the faculty of discrimination. And hidden deep within the higher mind, so to say, is a tiny doll that seems barely present but affects all the others: *ahamkara,* literally "that which makes me 'I,'" which I freely translate as ego. Ahamkara is the barrier between the transcendent Self and the little self that feels so isolated and fragmented.

Each of these levels of consciousness adds its own set of problems and confusion to the central question, Who am I? Each is a filter over the light of the Self. Ultimately, however, the cause of separateness is the ego-sense, the deeply embedded principle that our personal experience makes us separate from the rest of life.

This idea of levels of personality helps a good deal in understanding the Gita, so the image of dolls within dolls is a useful one to keep in mind. Later Indian philosophy gets quite technical about these levels, but the Gita avoids such complications. We can think simply of an inner self that wraps up all we think we are – our feelings, beliefs, desires, fears, aspirations, and ideals – and yet is separate from our real and innermost Self, the Atman.

The subtle body is a kind of mask – if you like, masks inside masks. We see the world through the masks we identify with, so identifying with the body brings with it all the others and imposes the crudest – that is, the most highly filtered – mode of knowing. Until Self-realization, we see most clearly when we identify only with the higher mind – in fact, seeing clearly is its job; it simply gets muddled and manacled by the body and the lower mind. To attain this state is itself a rare achievement, and brings a high measure of clarity and self-mastery.

Indian philosophy, following Shankara, calls such filters *upadhis,* which might be translated literally as "overlays." An upadhi is an apparent limitation imposed on one thing by another. The classical example is the horizon, which seems to limit the limitless sky but has no reality itself. Each level of personality – body, mind, buddhi, ego – is an upadhi, an artificial limitation that is real only insofar as we identify with it. Imagine being the Self at the core of our set of Russian dolls, looking out at the world through all those layers! No wonder we see as through a glass darkly – very darkly indeed.

The Gita is trying to tell us again that our life is really what our consciousness is. Everything we do and say and think is based upon the state of consciousness we have at the moment rather than on what is happening around us. When we are happy, we don't have any serious complaints against life; but if we're depressed, though we may have all the satisfactions that make for happiness, we feel empty inside, and life just doesn't seem worthwhile – not because the world has changed, but because there has been a change in consciousness.

Everything depends ultimately on consciousness, and our consciousness has been conditioned by countless limitations ranging from biological makeup to our upbringing, our education, our friends, the mass media, every blessed thing one can think of. All these make up the upadhis that hide our real Self.

One big problem is that this is our personality. We think it is who we are. Not only can we not imagine removing it, we don't really want to; we're rather fond of it, and imagine that others feel the same way. As I said earlier, this is a very limited view. A large number of people throughout the world believe they can express their personality by changing the color of the wallpaper or getting a new car. They forget that the word *personality* comes from the Latin *persona*: a mask. What we call personality is the mask of the ego, which hides the divine essence that is within. Our purpose in life is not to refine this mask, but to throw it away.

In this perspective we are all impostors, acting separate and self-centered and angry and playing all kinds of undesirable roles. Our real nature is to be naturally good, naturally kind, naturally big-hearted. It may not show, but all the conditioning that makes us selfish, self-willed, violent, and even cruel is a mask that can be taken away. That is why I find that image of a Russian doll so appealing: you can imagine taking off mask after mask until the innermost Self is revealed.

In a more homey comparison, this transformation is like coming in from a storm. First you take off your overcoat and hang it up carefully; then you take off your jacket, then your pullover. Similarly, you can slip out of your body and mind. It takes years to find the zippers, but once you know how, you can sit in meditation and quietly reach a stage where you can detach your identification with the physical body, then with the mind, and go deep into consciousness beyond time and space.

Once you make this discovery, when you want to use the mind during the day, you can simply slip it back on and zip it up. That may sound odd, because we think we need to use the mind all the time. In fact what is happening is that the mind is using us, running on and on with worries and anxieties and building castles in the air. It doesn't occur to us that we can slip it off and give it a rest – an extremely useful skill, as we shall see.

But the innermost covering, the sense of "I," is terribly difficult to remove. Since this is the final layer of separateness, of our very agency as an individual, removing it is a bit like lifting ourselves by our own bootstraps. In the end, that comes as something of a miracle – in traditional language, grace, from a power necessarily beyond our individual self.

Long before that state is attained, however, simply not identifying with body and mind brings unimaginable freedom. We can compare it playfully with riding a bicycle. Each of us is a kind of cyclist; the two wheels are the body and the mind, and we're on the seat with our feet on the pedals and hands gripping the bars. Do you remember the first time you tried to ride? I learned much later than most of you would have; we just didn't have many bikes in my village. (I made up for it by learning to ride an elephant.) While I was getting used to the ways of the bicycle, I remember wobbling down the path in my village and seeing a bullock cart coming towards me from a hundred yards or so away. Bullock carts are incredibly slow, so I really had plenty of time to decide what to do, but that didn't stop my hands from shaking and the wheels from going this way and that until I ran off the road. I didn't know who was more frightened, the bullock or me.

After some practice, however, I could cope even with heavy

traffic in a big city like Nagpur, which in those days meant cows, children, and carts crowding the street together with buses, cars, pedestrians, and other cyclists, most of them carrying outsized loads. You have to understand that kind of traffic – move around the cow, think like the children, know how the drivers drive. But once I learned all this, the bicycle became second nature. I could even look around and enjoy the sights; the bicycle had been forgotten.

It is just like that with knowing who you are. When you no longer identify with body or mind, you can move through life effortlessly – "no hands." You can make the right decisions without a tangle because you don't get all caught up in what to do, thinking one thing, feeling another, saying a third, and doing a fourth.

◈ *The Sticky Illusion*
of Separateness

HOW DID WE come to identify ourselves so completely with the physical urges and private predilections that make up such a small fragment of who we are? Why can't we shake off this nightmare of separateness – one party against another, one nation against another, one race against another, one individual against another? The Gita's answer is simple but far-reaching: this is our biological legacy. When we are driven by anger, fear, lust, or greed, it is not hard to recognize the conditioning of our evolutionary past. It is this conditioning that makes us identify ourselves with body and mind – makes us think that is what we are.

Sanskrit calls this obsessive identification maya, the creative power of illusion that is implicit in the human mind. But "illusion" is misleading, for so long as we see life this way, this illusion is very real.

Maya explains why we see what is not there and fail to see what is. The word has been connected with the English word *magic,* which may not be sound etymology but makes a fruitful image. The main principle in magic is to divert the attention of the audience. If I can get you to give complete attention to my left hand, I can do anything I like with my right and you won't notice. Similarly, to conceal the Atman, no one has to hide it under a blanket; that would be very poor magic. The best magicians can hide something simply by making us look somewhere else. And that's just what maya does: it conceals the Self within us by assuring us that what will satisfy us lies "out there," just around the corner – in physical attractions, in the allure of power or prestige, in the promise of romantic love. That's why we always go looking for fulfillment in changing situations – in the flux of appearances, the world of the senses, the world of change.

I can give a simple illustration of maya from my village in South India, where we used to play a game probably thousands of years old. The performer sits by the roadside with three coconut half-shells upside down on a piece of cloth, shows bystanders a little ball, and says, "I'm going to put this ball under one of these shells, and then I'm going to move the shells around in front of your eyes while you watch. My hands are so fast they'll make your head spin. If you think your eyes are faster, you place some money in front of the shell that has the ball. If you're right, I'll give you double – but if you guess wrong, I get to keep what you bet."

Then he puts the ball under one of the shells and moves

them all around in a blur while we watch like hawks. "Now who wants to bet?" There would always be someone to step forward and put his money down – and every time, when the shell was lifted, there would be nothing underneath.

I never saw anybody win that game, but we always felt so sure. I don't think it ever occurred to me that the ball might actually end up in the palm of his hand. Raman would try and lose; then Shankaran would say, "I saw the ball, I really saw it, just under the first shell." He feels so certain that he puts down his quarter, but there's nothing there. One by one, each places his bet, loses his money, and stands aside to watch the next fellow – and then goes and bets again.

Sometimes a performer like this would come to school during lunchtime, spread out his mat, and start his spiel. Old-timers would warn the first-year students, "We've played this; you will never win." Deaf ears. They would go, play, and lose everything, and then next year they too would tell the next batch of students, "Don't play that game. You will never win." And of course the newcomers go on to play and lose.

This is maya: some magic spell that makes us think we see joy where it is not and fail to see joy where it is. You put your money down and maya makes you feel absolutely positive the ball is there. Every time. It may not work with Rosalind, but it's sure to work with Juliet – and if not Juliet, well, maybe Viola or Miranda . . .

That's the kind of game that maya plays, and as long as we

have personal desires to fulfill, the Gita says, we cannot help getting caught in it. Only when we are detached – when we cease asking life to give us something for nothing – will we stop and think, "Wait, no one has ever won this," and refuse to put our money down. In life, of course, even more than money, we put our feelings down – our hopes, our needs, our love. And when feelings are the stakes, they get hurt – and that is just what maya likes, because hurt feelings keep us in the game. "Just one more time . . ."

Superimposition

We can think of maya as imposing the characteristics of the container on the contents – the characteristics of the physical organism on the Self.

For an absurd example, suppose you asked me what breakfast cereal is and I replied, "It's a waxy cardboard box with advertising on it"? If you believed that, trying to eat your cereal the next morning would be a frustrating experience – though perhaps not less nutritious than what is inside the box, considering the kind of stuff I see for sale in the supermarket. In fact, supermarket shelves are a lot like maya: countless containers all trying to look different, but much the same inside except that some are sweeter.

It sounds absurd, but mistaking the contents for the container like this is exactly what we do every day when we yield to physical urges. In Indian philosophy this is called *adhyaropa,* superimposition: layer on layer of mistaken identity, built up over millions of years of evolution as consciousness develops in higher and higher organisms. We have seen that in sankhya, everything is prakriti and prakriti is essentially energy. What differentiates this energy into apparently different things is their "name and form": in Sanskrit, *namarupa,* the essence of a thing and its material substance. "Name and form" is what takes us in and makes us believe we are separate individuals when there is really only one Self in billions of forms. Namarupa is the appearance; what we need to remember is the essence, which is divine.

When our niece Meera was young, what she enjoyed most about Christmas morning was not so much the presents as unwrapping them. All those colored papers and ribbons gave her endless pleasure; what was inside was almost incidental. When we allow ourselves to be drawn solely by physical attractions and the promise of physical satisfaction, we are behaving exactly the same way: getting absorbed in the wrapping and ribbons without being aware that there is something precious within. One of the sights that rends my heart is two people who say they are fond of each other when they are only admiring the packaging. For a while they can entertain themselves with fancy paper and ribbons, but sooner or later they begin to get bored, and that spells the end of joy.

This is the fantasy of maya: imposing the joy and wisdom within us to the play in the phenomenal world. "Interest rates have gone up to twelve percent! In six years I can double my money, and if this goes on I can retire to the Bahamas . . ." This is fantasyland: attributing the fulfillment inside you to twelve percent interest and a Bahamas beach.

Each of us is an expert in this art. "If only I could get entangled with that person, wouldn't life be wonderful? Jealousy in the morning, some resentments in the afternoon, disillusionment in the evening – what a day!" In plain language, this is what most relationships based on personal desires amount to, which shows just how practical abstract-sounding ideas like superimposition actually are.

Strangely enough, we are a bit illogical about this. After a while, when we see we're not getting what we are looking for, we don't turn inwards; we look for some other object to impose this fantasy on. If it is not the Bahamas, let's try Monte Carlo; that's where the real action is. If it's not Joan or Johnny, why not Linda or Leonard? I have met quite a few people who went on like this all their lives.

In relationships, superimposition results in imposing our will on others. In Western mysticism this is called self-will, which is an extremely useful concept. Self-will is the universal tendency to put oneself first and everybody else last – to insist on my way, my ideas, my beliefs, my happiness, no matter who or what gets in the way.

While we think of ourselves as separate, some measure of self-will is unavoidable. But self-will is a vicious circle: the more we indulge it, the more separate we feel, and the more separate we feel, the more we are driven to preserve ourselves and our interests at any cost.

Sadly, material progress seems to have aggravated this cycle. Despite the technological achievements of the last hundred years – perhaps even encouraged by them, to the extent technology has facilitated separateness – extreme states of self-will are increasingly considered normal, making lasting relationships between man and woman almost impossible.

To the extent we are self-willed, we cannot escape imposing our needs on those around us. It is almost as if we make a plastic mold of our needs – physical, emotional, even intellectual – and then go about looking for people we can force that mold onto. If they struggle, we say, "Don't spoil my life." Then we expect them to behave according to the mold we have made. And when they don't – which is rather predictable – we get upset and object, "You're not being true to yourself!" Which means, "How you agitate me! Why don't you try to behave like my image of you?"

Of course, since self-will is universal, others are trying at the same time to force their own molds on us. It's a simultaneous superimposition. In a Hindu marriage both the man and the woman have garlands, and at the auspicious moment they exchange them: she puts her garland around his neck; he puts his around hers. Superimposition is like that: you stand facing each other, raise your plastic molds, and put them on each other; and if there are features that don't quite fit, you just press and pull to make them fit, even if the other person complains.

Most of us have a collection of these molds in a kind of trophy room in the mind. Whenever we get into a personal relationship, we pick out one that seems right and put it on the person we fancy. The relationship is really with the mold! We expect that person to behave in accordance with the mold, and when they behave like themselves instead, we are thrown into confusion. "What is all this? Why does life have to be so difficult? I don't seem to be able to relate to her, she can't relate to me, what has gone wrong?" All that is wrong is this game of superimposition.

The opposite game is called *apohata* in Sanskrit: breaking the mold, not the ones you have of others but the mold you have of yourself. This hurts, of course. It's much more appealing to go about taking a hammer to the molds of others. But that won't do; they will just get made again, because they are constructed by your own mold of yourself.

All of us have an image of ourselves which we'll swear by bell, book, and candle is absolutely correct. We're not even aware that we have such an image, since we view the world through it. It's a dreadfully accurate diagnosis: we don't really see other people; we see them through our conditioning. If we could only see ourselves as we really are, not separate but part of the whole tree of life, and could translate this into our daily life, the mold would fall away. Only then do we discover that the Self in us is the same as the Self in every other creature, which is seeing life as it is:

> They alone see truly who see the Lord the same in every
> creature, who see the Deathless in the hearts of all that
> die. (13:27)

Moha

Maya, then, is the illusion of separateness. The confusion it causes is called *moha*, which is sometimes translated as infatuation. But that is misleading, because infatuation comes and goes. Moha doesn't go; it only becomes more intense the longer we indulge it. Moha is delusion, confusion, hallucination. The idea that money can bring fulfillment, for example, is a hallucination people have been pursuing since time began. No one has ever found it to be true, but that doesn't prevent the next generation from chasing the same mirage. When the delusion gets overpowering, those under its spell might as well have dollar signs on their pupils; they see everything through this one obsession. Show them a beautiful landscape and they think, "Ah, a subdivision!" or "Wouldn't this be a good place for a luxury hotel?"

Moha's special domain, however, is physical attraction – the kind of physical or emotional entanglement between two people that holds within itself the seed of its own destruction. In the early days of a relationship, getting entangled with the object of our desire brings such pleasure that we never notice how we are being conditioned. We can't see anything clearly, can't act wisely, can't really act in freedom at all; it's like living in a dream. But it is the nature of a compulsion to satisfy less and less as the activity becomes automatic. Then it's only a matter of time before attraction turns into repulsion. Each of us must have observed this sometime or other: two people who couldn't be apart even for a day reach a point where they can't stand each other's sight.

Obsessive relationships have been a staple of romantic fiction for centuries. For some reason, no matter how tragic the end of Tristan and Iseult or of Heathcliff and Cathy, such passion attracts us, even against our better judgment. One author I used to read often, Somerset Maugham, made a brilliant but disturbing study of the negative side of this kind of relationship in his novel *Of Human Bondage*. (Christine and I went to see the first film version, which made Bette Davis a star.) The title is perfectly chosen. Philip Carey, a medical student who dreams of becoming an artist, finds himself caught in a baffling attraction to an unappealing, manipulative waitress called Mildred – a not-so-*belle dame sans merci*. The more she refuses and uses him, the more obsessed he becomes. He doesn't like Mildred, doesn't respect her, doesn't even want to think about her, but he cannot rest until he marries her. The subsequent decline – of him, of her, of all the relationships the obsession pulls into its vortex – is heartbreaking. This was the book that introduced me to Maugham, and even as a student I could recognize it as a great novel. But the story upset me terribly, just because of this utter inability to judge any situation or exercise self-control.

Moha is like a drug that uses our own powers to bind us. We want to believe our delusions because they promise to make up for what we think we lack. But as my grandmother used to say, "You can't blame a mango tree for not giving you bananas." Our needs are not physical; how can they be satisfied in physical ways?

> Delusion arises from the duality of attraction and aversion, Arjuna; every creature is deluded by these from birth. But those who have freed themselves from all wrongdoing are firmly established in worship of me. Their actions are pure, and they are free from the delusion caused by the pairs of opposites. (7:27–28)

The Glue of the Senses

The Gita explains moha in an intriguing way, based on the nature of sensory experience. In the Gita's view, remember, senses and sense objects are two aspects of a single event in consciousness. They exist together; they cannot exist separately. They have an integral relationship of their own, which is neither pleasant nor unpleasant but simply *is* – unless the human observer jumps in, which unfortunately we cannot help doing when we identify ourselves with the body

and senses. Then we project our personal needs onto our experiences, which charges them with emotion. The result is a
very sticky attachment of either attraction or aversion – "I like
this, I don't like that."

This is probably easiest to see where it is most practical: in
purely physical attraction between two people. Today this
sort of thing is called "chemistry," a surprisingly good term.
Hydrogen atoms have a spare electron each, oxygen needs
two; put them together and in an instant they are locked into
one. This kind of reaction has nothing to do with love, but it's
inescapable when the only factor is physical appeal.

In all such cases – not just between two people, but in any
kind of sensory attraction – the Gita asks simply, "Why
should you jump in? This is a relationship between *things,*
between senses and sense objects; you are not involved":

> When the senses contact sense objects, a person experi-
> ences cold or heat, pleasure or pain. These experiences
> are fleeting; they come and go. Bear them patiently,
> Arjuna. Those who are unaffected by these changes,
> who are the same in pleasure and pain, are truly wise
> and fit for immortality. (2:14–15)

The other day I was watching two dogs chasing each other
around the lawn while the men who took care of them looked
on like doting parents. The dogs were having the time of their

lives; we human beings were irrelevant bystanders. But what if Michael and Stuart, not content with watching, had got down on all fours to join in? Ridiculous, but that's just what *moha* amounts to. It's a matter between senses and sense objects; there is no reason for us to get involved at all.

As long as we entangle ourselves in this relationship, the Gita says, we are going to see life divided. We cannot escape duality. Whatever we do, whatever we experience, there has to be an opposite: joy cannot exist without sorrow, pleasure without pain, good without evil, and so on. However much we want to separate them, however fervently we want to think we can have one without the other, these are conjoined twins.

This insight is the special contribution of the Gita. We cannot see life as only pleasure; we can see it only as pleasure and pain, and as a result the mind is in constant upheaval, up and down in response to how it labels the experiences of the moment. This is the real appeal of pleasure: we are attracted to pleasure because it excites the mind. In fact, this up and down movement in consciousness is precisely what the "lower mind" is. That is why stilling the mind brings us to a state beyond pleasure and pain, which the Upanishads call *ananda:* neither sensation or emotion, but a higher state of consciousness altogether.

When we wake up into this state and look back upon past moments of pleasure, we can see there was really no pleasure in those moments, only sensations. But if I identify myself with my body and senses, then whenever my senses come in contact with sensory experiences, what they experience I attribute to myself.

As long as we are conditioned by pleasure and pain, the Gita says, the mind has to keep going up and down; and as long as the mind is going up and down, we cannot see clearly. In order to see the world as it is, to see people as they really are, we need to view everything with complete equanimity. Then there is no question of vision being disturbed by something because I don't like it, or distorted by some event because it doesn't accord with my expectations.

The Costs of Delusion

Unfortunately, the fog of delusion is our normal state, and Sri Krishna uses some of his strongest language to persuade Arjuna where this leads. It is we ourselves who plunge ourselves into suffering, very much like Philip Carey, not so much intentionally as because of this blind attachment to sensory pleasure. The problem is not the senses or enjoying the world they present to us: there is no problem if, as William Blake says, we "kiss the joy as it flies." It is focusing on ourselves – clinging to these experiences, trying to hold on to them and squeeze out any pleasure they offer – that glues us to the ups and downs of pleasure and pain.

In other words, the root problem is not sensory indulgence, in which most of us probably consider ourselves reasonably restrained. The root problem lies in the mind: thinking about sensory satisfaction, talking about it, hearing about it, reading about it, day in and day out. Most of us have friends who are happy to contribute to this situation; almost everyone seems to enjoy talking about food or drink or sex or material possessions. But this natural propensity is compounded by the mass media, which saturate us with messages about sense pleasure in movies and shows, popular music, magazines and books, newspapers and tabloids, and advertising, advertising, advertising. All this leads to the rousing of desires that cannot be fulfilled, which in the long run can lead to loss of judgment and a life that is thrown away.

If this sounds grim, it is only a subdued paraphrase of two verses which Gandhi says haunted him from the day he first read them as a student in London. In Sanskrit they are terrible; each word is like a depth charge:

> When you keep thinking about sense objects, attachment comes. Attachment breeds desire, the lust of possession that burns to anger. Anger clouds the judgment; you can no longer learn from past mistakes. Lost is the power to choose between what is wise and what is unwise, and your life is utter waste. (2:62–63)

It is only on a very few occasions like this that Sri Krishna speaks with utmost severity to warn of the dangers lurking even in pursuits we consider harmless. In particular, we need to be aware how much of the mass media is based on a rather lurid appeal to the senses, because it all goes into the mind. An immense amount of money and talent today is spent on finding words and images that appeal to the most primitive instincts, conditioning us to go on thinking about sensory pleasure whether awake or asleep. And when the clamor of the senses becomes rebellious, I don't think any political demonstration could be more vocal. When they demand satisfaction, they won't let us sleep: they'll come up in dreams, they'll come up in waking life.

Of course, there are books and movies and even television shows that provide good entertainment and good education. The point is to be able to choose. With junk food so readily available, most of us have learned to be selective about what we put into our mouths; why not be careful about what we let into our minds?

So Krishna is urging, Don't make a habit of dwelling upon sensory stimulation. Don't read about it, don't watch movies about it, don't listen to songs about it, don't talk about it, because gradually you will get so attached to those thoughts that you can't get them out of your head – and then the desire slowly arises to find out for yourself.

When this happens, there seems to be almost a law that if we are driven by the desire for a particular experience, sooner or later we will find ourselves in places where that desire can be fulfilled. When you keep hearing about drugs, for example, thinking about them, talking to people who are using them, the day will come when you find yourself in a situation where you can get some substance or other and try it out. When the desire comes, the will begins to follow; and when will and desire join together, the deed is done.

At that time, nothing will convince you that this will not bring you what you want. Every one of us has gone through this stage, when friends warn us that we are about to make a big mistake and we assure them, "No, you're wrong. It's very clear that this is the way to love and happiness" – only to find, sometimes the very next morning, that we have fallen into a trap. The senses promise everything, but they simply can't deliver. Of their nature, sensations are superficial; our needs go much, much deeper.

The progression Sri Krishna describes in these verses is not confined to a particular desire. Our whole civilization seems to be built on whipping up desire – for this, for that, for everything under the sun that someone wants to sell. Each day we are bombarded with promises that acquiring things and experiencing sensations will make us happy, and since they cannot – because happiness can only be found within – frustration cannot help building up below the surface of consciousness. Life is promising all this and not delivering! Anger, hostility, even fury build up without our understanding why, and often they erupt for no apparent reason: "road rage" is a prime example.

And Krishna doesn't stop here. This anger and frustration goes on building to a fog of utter confusion: moha. I think it is St. Paul who defined confusion as doing what we should not do and neglecting to do what we should. It's a state I see every day in the papers and on the news.

And gradually there comes the loss of the precious faculty to learn from previous mistakes. All of us are fallible; everyone makes mistakes trying to hold life to promises it can't fulfill. But unless we learn from our mistakes, we are going to go on repeating them. Without the capacity to learn from experience, we simply cannot grow; we will continue to get trapped in situations that have only led to sorrow.

The Bond of Attachment

Moha reminds me of those superglues that can bond anything to anything else forever – the ones with dire warning labels that can't seem to keep users out of the emergency room. Superglues are chemically the same, I believe, but moha has a different adhesive for each level of personality: one kind to glue the senses to the body, a second to bond mind to senses, a third to stick the intellect and the will to the mind, and a special adhesive to glue the ego to the whole collection. Imagine those Russian dolls glued together like this! No wonder so much work is required to get free.

Indians like to illustrate this strange adhesive with stories about jackfruit, which grows in abundance in my native Kerala. The fruits of a jack tree are huge – easily as long as my arm – and when they ripen, they fill the air with a heady fragrance that attracts people from all around. (And cows. Jackfruit is to cows what ice cream is to children.) Inside each fruit are sweet, golden-hued pods with a lot of sticky milk around the seeds – so sticky that if you get it on your hands, you won't be able to pry your palms apart.

Everyone in Kerala knows this about jackfruit, but people from other parts of India are often unfamiliar with its ways. So when a visitor arrives from out of state – especially from a big city like Bombay or Delhi – mischievous children like to offer them the traditional plate of jackfruit pods for refreshment. The guests dig in, and then the children ask innocently, "Would you like some more?" And the only reply they get is "Mmh," because the guests find their lips stuck together, and maybe their hands as well. They sit there baffled, more and more embarrassed, while the children giggle and go on asking question after question.

If you try this with a Keralite, however, he or she will ask, "Where is the coconut oil?" That is how jackfruit is usually served, with a little bowl of oil on the side. Before we touch the fruit, we dip our fingers into the oil and smear some on our hands and lips like sunscreen. Then we can eat all we want and still recite Shakespeare if we choose.

Attachment to body, mind, senses, and ego is like that sticky juice: we enjoy, but then we're stuck. The secret the Gita will offer is not coconut oil but detachment – not from other people, but from ourselves. If we know who we are, we won't get stuck to these components of a false personality; then we can enjoy life in freedom.

This brings us at last to the heart of the Gita: how to turn all these insights into practice, which is the purpose of yoga.

CHAPTER SIX

◇ *The Meaning of Yoga*

IN THE GITA, the spiritual life has two aspects, theory and practice. The theoretical aspect is called sankhya; the practical aspect is yoga. In a beautiful verse, Sri Krishna says that only children separate theory from practice; sankhya and yoga are one:

> The immature think that sankhya and yoga, knowledge
> and action, are different, but the wise see them as the
> same. Anyone established in one of these paths will
> attain the rewards of both. (5:4)

To understand, we need to practice, and it is only through practice that true understanding comes. This sounds paradoxical, but isn't it the same with any art or skill? The spiritual life in particular is an unfolding study, in which practice and understanding go on deepening each other without end.

Often there is a gulf that yawns between theory and practice. People who write about the mind cannot control their mind; people who write about the body cannot control their senses. I vividly remember watching a cancer specialist study the X-ray of a diseased lung while smoking a cigarette. As St. Francis of Assisi says, our knowledge is only as deep as our action.

Sankhya here is not just theory; it is also a particular theory, based on the ideas behind the Gita's presentation of sanatana dharma. At the beginning of the Gita, Krishna summarizes these ideas in beautiful poetry and then says, "You have heard the intellectual explanation of sankhya, Arjuna; now listen to the principles of yoga" (2:39). We too have reviewed the basic ideas; now it is time to return to the war within: the split in consciousness, introduced in chapter 1, which is the theme of the Bhagavad Gita.

I have characterized this division in various ways, because it manifests itself differently depending on the level of consciousness from which it is viewed. It is essentially a split between the separate, self-centered personality that is rooted in body consciousness – the small self, the ego – and the Atman, the higher or transcendental Self. I have also called it a tug of war between the selfish and the selfless, between the higher mind and the lower mind, between wisdom and ignorance. In practical terms, it is the tension between an upward pull towards freedom from biological conditioning and the downward pull that holds us back.

We can picture this split as a V, dividing the separate side of personality from the universal. The top of this V represents the world of everyday experience. We think this is the whole of life, but it is insignificant compared with what lies below the surface: preconscious awareness, the subconscious, and the vast regions of the unconscious mind.

This division is present in every one of us; that is the human condition. At first it may be narrow, but whenever we yield to the pull of the body, senses, mind, and ego, the split becomes wider and wider. And although it is only visible at the surface, in behavior, it runs through personality right to the core like a slice through those Russian dolls. How to heal that split – how to make ourselves whole – is the essential challenge in life and the very heart of the Bhagavad Gita.

Where the split is slight, a person will be secure and selfless, easily aware of the needs of others. Such a person is probably one in a million. For the rest of us the division gapes much wider. Whenever we identify ourselves with any desire for personal pleasure or profit, the split widens. When these two sides of ourselves are pulling against each other most of the time, there is likely to be conflict everywhere. Then emotional difficulties multiply, not only in number but in intensity. Conflicts become more frequent; peace and security are banished from our lives.

At the top of this V, where the gap is widest, you can see that there's no support. That's what superficial living means: resting on no support without realizing the turmoil beneath. There are good people who can honestly say that they haven't experienced the turmoil and frustration and despair that most of us feel at one time or another. They will tell you cheerfully, "We're getting on well enough. We have made some money; we own our own home and have sent the children to university; we've even traveled around the world once or twice." My sympathy goes out to such people. It is much better to be frustrated, I would say, than to be unaware of this inner conflict and not grow.

Years ago I saw an article by a distinguished psychiatrist arguing that every human being harbors a tendency to mental illness – a hairbreadth fissure that can split apart under the stress of circumstances. One illustration he gave was disloyalty, which might manifest itself at first only as a tendency to vacillate – not merely in relationships but over values. Under stress, a tiny fracture like this can crack without warning: a person might reverse loyalties, or a good man commit a crime. Because there are two sides to the split in consciousness, however, the reverse can happen too. We see this in *A Tale of Two Cities*, when the dissolute lawyer Sydney Carton chooses to die in the place of a man he hates for the sake of the woman they both love.

Today, vacillation is often prized; disloyalty is even considered a sign of the capacity to change and grow. Yet in spite of such euphemistic interpretations, most of us know from experience what strength it gives us to be loyal to a friend or to values we cherish, and how poorly we think of ourselves when those loyalties break under pressure. It is said that a ship is tested not in calm weather but in stormy seas. Similarly, integrity of personality is not tested when the going is easy; it is tested when we face provocation and our deepest values are challenged.

Through superimposition, all of these internal weaknesses are projected onto people and events outside us. Ultimately, the Gita would say, all the resentment that we feel against others is really directed against ourselves, against our own drawbacks, insecurities, and inadequacies – the lower self against the higher. When we burst out at someone with no apparent provocation, it is because of this split in the deeper regions of our own consciousness. Whenever we act on negative feelings like this, the split becomes wider, making resentment even more likely the next time someone crosses our expectations.

What is the source of all this division? Those who are biochemically oriented might lay responsibility on the body; others will lay it at the threshold of society. The question reminds me of a strange story I heard when we lived in Oakland, about a house actually sliding down the Berkeley hills. The tenant sued the owner, the owner sued the contractor, the contractor sued the engineer, the engineer sued the surveyor; the lawyers must have had a field day. We can imagine a similar suit here too. The body is first to be accused; after all, it's the only party that's visible. But it can sue the senses. "How could I be responsible for this? I'm inert. I don't make decisions; don't take it out on me." When the senses are called to the witness stand, they object, "We don't have any choice in these matters; we're just puppets. We listen to the mind." By the time the mind is brought to witness, its defense looks shaky. But the mind is a slick customer. "I may look guilty, I admit, but the culprit is not me. It's the ego. He's the only real agent." Here the mystics of all religions agree: behind all our difficulties and conflicts and sufferings, the party that is actually responsible is self-will, ahamkara, the innermost level of personality, which sits behind the curtain and pulls the strings.

I once saw a clever British comedy by the Boulting Brothers dedicated "to those who got away with it." In this caper, it is the ego who gets away with it, at least for the time being. Body and mind pay the penalties, but in the end it is we who suffer, by becoming estranged from ourselves. This is the greatest tragedy I can imagine, since being alienated from ourselves means being cut off from the rest of life.

Yoga

Near our home is a beauty parlor with a sign proclaiming, "Say goodbye to split ends!" I had to ask Christine what it means. But I would immediately understand a meditation hall that put up a similar sign: "Say goodbye to split consciousness." That is the real purpose of this much-misunderstood discipline called yoga.

Yoga is both end and means, both the goal and the path: the state of unified consciousness and any of the various ways of realizing it. Eventually these approaches evolved into separate schools, one of which, hatha yoga, is practically synonymous with yoga in the West. The Bhagavad Gita, however, was composed before these seemingly watertight divisions arose. It is a text on yoga, full stop. Its principles are general enough to support all schools of yoga that aim at the realization of the Atman, and every traditional school in India reveres it as a basic text.

The word *yoga* is related to the English word *yoke*; it signifies a binding together of parts that have been torn asunder, a reunification, integration, union. In a practical sense it signifies full health in body, mind, and spirit, just as the word *health* carries the root meaning "to be whole."

But this can be misleading, for yoga does not mean union with components of personality like the body and mind but complete identification with the Atman, which uses body and mind as instruments. That is why one famous commentator on yoga, Bhoja, says that yoga can really be called *viyoga*, "disunion": the art of prying ourselves free from this sticky obsession that we are body and mind by realizing who we truly are. What he is trying to say is that when the Self is entirely freed from the limitations of body and mind, it attains the unitive state.

In this sense, our ordinary glued-together personality is like a cling peach, with skin and flesh and pit all stuck together. The state of yoga can be compared to a freestone peach: one side is the body, the other side is the mind; pry them apart and the stone just falls out. In practice, this happens in stages: first we discover that the body is our external instrument, then that the mind is our internal instrument. Finally, in samadhi, we discover we are the operator of these instruments, the Self.

In traditional language, in this state there is "continuous awareness of the unity of Atman and Brahman" – that is, continuous awareness of the unity of life. This is not just philosophy. When this division is healed completely, the mark of it is unconditional love of all life:

> Those who are established in themselves see the Self in
> every creature and all creation in the Self. With
> consciousness unified through meditation, they see
> everything with an equal eye. . . . Feeling the joys and
> sorrows of others as their own, they have attained the
> highest state of spiritual awareness. (6:29, 32)

To be divided is to be tense; to be united is to be relaxed. To be divided is disloyalty; to be united is complete loyalty. To be divided is gross insecurity; to be united is unshakable security. To be divided is to be fragile in the face of life's most important challenges; to be united is to win the goal in life whatever the challenges, whatever the obstacles.

In other words, practicing yoga means that health, security, creativity, insight, and spiritual awareness all grow together. We don't have to try to solve one little problem after another, which is the way most of us go about it. Faced with a whole alphabet of problems, we start with A, Apathy, and try to deal with it, and while we are wrestling with A, B through Z run wild. Then we turn to B and Apathy gets loose again, and so on. Chasing the alphabet like this is a long, laborious, frustrating process because there is really no end to the problems the mind can create. Life is not long enough for getting all of these problems out of the way, even if we could do it systematically. So Sri Krishna says, "Don't just try to tackle the problems the mind creates. Go to the root: tackle the mind":

> Those who follow the path of yoga, resolving deep
> within themselves to seek me alone, attain singleness of
> purpose. For those who lack resolution, the decisions
> of life are many-branched and endless. (2:41)

Skill in Action

It is helpful to remember that although the Gita is a manual for every kind of spiritual seeker, Arjuna is a man of action, immersed in the problems of everyday life. That is why so much of the Gita focuses on the practical benefits of yoga, which Sri Krishna sums up as "skill in action":

When consciousness is unified, all vain anxiety is left behind. There is no cause for worry, whether things go well or ill. Therefore, Arjuna, devote yourself to the disciplines of yoga, for yoga is skill in action. (2:50)

The key to this skill is an even mind – a mind that is immune to the ups and downs of fortune, success and failure, honor and dishonor, pleasure and pain, all of which are the effects of a divided mind in daily life:

> Those whose minds are swept away by the pursuit of pleasure and power are incapable of following the supreme goal and will not attain samadhi. The scriptures describe the three gunas, but you should be free from the action of the gunas, established in eternal truth, self-controlled, without any sense of duality or the desire to acquire and hoard. . . .
>
> You have the right to work, but never to the fruit of work. You should never engage in action for the sake of reward, nor should you long for inaction. Perform work in this world, Arjuna, as a man established within himself – without selfish attachments, and alike in success and defeat. For yoga is perfect evenness of mind. (2:44–45, 47–48)

Most of us cannot help letting our minds react to circumstances, surging up and down in waves of excitement or depression depending on how we think things are going for us.

To heal this root division in consciousness, we have to learn to make the mind steady and one-pointed no matter what is happening outside. As long as the mind is swinging back and forth, the Gita says, we are at the mercy of events outside us, like puppets with the world pulling our strings. The purpose of yoga is to prevent this wild swinging of the mind by keeping the mind in equilibrium throughout the day.

I like to think of this as a kind of homeostasis for the mind, akin to the body's capacity to maintain essential processes such as heart rate and body temperature despite changes in the external environment. When you run fast, for example, your heart rate jumps to keep pumping enough blood for that level of activity. After thirty minutes, your heart may be beating twice as fast as normal. Your body needs that rate while running, but suppose that when you finish your run there is no way for the pulse to come down. You wouldn't live long with your heart racing at one hundred and fifty! The load on the heart would be terrible. Fortunately, in a healthy man or woman the body needs only ten minutes or so for the pulse to return to seventy-five. The body has evolved feedback mechanisms to maintain this kind of balance. The Gita is implying that the mind too needs homeostasis – some way to stay even through life's ups and downs.

In the body, homeostatic regulation is unconscious. We don't have to tell the heart to return to normal; it has developed its own way of knowing. Perhaps someday this capacity will evolve in the mind as well, but until then we have to train the mind to stay in balance until it learns to do so automatically – which, again, is much like learning a physical skill. Walking on two legs is an incredible skill; it takes a lot of work to master it. But once learned, the skill is pushed into the unconscious; we don't need to keep thinking about it. That is just what yoga does for the mind: the higher mind learns to monitor the lower, providing a higher level of feedback.

In this way the mind can be trained to maintain balance when it is exposed to anger or fear or any other negative emotion. Just as a healthy body maintains a normal temperature in heat and cold, the mind can learn to stay calm and kind in the face of provocation. Of course, for a while the mind will be upset: the capacity to feel deeply is not impaired but strengthened. But you will not act compulsively under the goad of fear or anger. You will see clearly and compassionately, and in a short while your mind will be even again, which means it will remain at its best for dealing with whatever situation it is in.

One of the easiest ways to learn this kind of self-regulating balance is to lower the threshold of likes and dislikes. This is one way to go to the root of emotional problems: rather than work on problems with a mind that is subject to those problems, make the mind independent of ups and downs. Don't go on doing things just because you like them, especially if they don't need to be done or are even harmful; and don't avoid doing things just because you dislike them, particularly if they need to be done or will benefit others.

Catering to likes and dislikes is the road to turmoil and the very opposite of yoga. When you have hardly any likes and dislikes, you are free to enjoy everything and equal to every situation. You have choices everywhere, so you never feel trapped; whatever the circumstances, you can break out. Simply knowing that life can't hold you hostage brings a lasting sense of joy long before perfect yoga is attained. Therefore, the Gita says in famous lines,

> On this path effort never goes to waste, and there is no
> failure. Even a little effort toward spiritual awareness
> will protect you from the greatest fear. (2:40)

Nevertheless, the ultimate goal of yoga is lofty, not at all easy to attain. In a famous commentary on yoga, Shankara says succinctly, "Yoga is samadhi." Precise and to the point. Even a little practice of yoga brings great benefits, but we cannot call ourselves yogis until we attain Self-realization. Until then we are spiritual aspirants.

The Three Yogas

The Bhagavad Gita offers three major paths to this ultimate goal: karma yoga, the way of work or selfless action; jnana yoga, the way of wisdom; and bhakti yoga, the way of love or devotion. Theoretically it is possible to reach the unitive state along any of these paths. It's like a freeway with three lanes. But if you call the Cosmic Patrol and ask for the traffic situation, they will tell you that two of those lanes are more like narrow, unpaved mountain roads, the kind with a lot of hairpin turns and no guardrails. Sri Krishna does praise all three, but Arjuna keeps asking, "Which is best?"

Jnana yoga, the path of wisdom or knowledge, appeals to many people today because we are so intellectually oriented. But jnana has very little to do with the intellect. It transcends the intellect; it is direct, experiential knowledge of the unity of life, attained by progressively seeing through the layers of delusion that glue us to the body and mind – something that is simple to talk about but almost impossible to do. Sri Krishna describes the goal and qualifications of this path in beautiful verses:

> As for those who seek the transcendental Reality, without name, without form, contemplating the Unmanifested, beyond the reach of thought and of feeling, with their senses subdued and mind serene and striving for the good of all beings, they too will verily come unto me. (12:3–4)

In other words, anyone who would like to follow this path needs trained senses, a still mind, and no identification with the body – which is to say that even to get started, one must almost have reached the goal. It reminds me of that old canard: "You can't get a job unless you belong to the union, and you can't join the union unless you have a job." If you can practice jnana yoga, you don't need it, and if you need it, you won't be able to practice it. This is not a comment on jnana yoga, but on how impossible this path is for ordinary people like you and me to follow in today's sense-saturated culture. It is like climbing Mount Everest up a ninety-degree slope.

There have been outstanding examples of jnana yogis in every religious tradition, and because the nature of this path is to strip away inessentials, they sound very much alike: the teachings of Shankara in eighth-century India and of Meister Eckhart in medieval Germany often seem interchangeable. In modern times India had a spiritual giant named Sri Ramana Maharshi, who attained complete illumination in a matter of hours at the age of sixteen. But these are not dry intellects; this deep wisdom goes hand in hand with love of God. To know is to love, and to love is to act:

United with Brahman, ever joyful, beyond the reach of desire and sorrow, they have equal regard for every living creature and attain supreme devotion to me. By loving me they come to know me truly; then they know my glory and enter into my boundless being. All their acts are performed in my service, and through my grace they win eternal life. (18:54–56)

Karma Yoga

The second path is karma yoga, the way of self-less action. This way appeals to those who want to make some contribution to the welfare of others, but karma yoga is more than service. Service – work that benefits others – *is* necessary for every human being, the Gita maintains; it is incumbent on us to give back to life as we take from it. But this becomes yoga only when it is selfless: when we forget ourselves in that work and desire nothing from it for ourselves, not even recognition or appreciation. When we learn to act in this way, egotism shrinks and separateness gradually dissolves.

Such selfless service is rare. Much more common – among those who help the world at all – are those who do good but need some kind of recognition or reward. Such people have benefited the world enormously, so these words are not meant at their expense. The question is simply what effect this work has on them. If it loosens egotism, pride, and the bonds of separateness, it can be called karma yoga, but not if it is making these bonds stronger.

The word *karma* comes from the Sanskrit word for doing, and refers not only to physical action but to words and even thoughts. Anything that has an effect in the field of prakriti, whether the physical world or the mind, is karma. Even when we are thinking, we are acting. Angry thoughts, for example, affect not only ourselves but those around us. Just go and sit near an angry person for a while; by the time you leave, you will feel you had been squeezed dry.

So the word *karma* means not only actions but the consequences of action, in the fullest sense of the word. Every action has effects which go on to become causes, in an endless chain of cause and effect. The virtue of karma yoga is that when we act without thought of self, there is no channel for the results of our actions to act on us again. Every human being has an immense load of past karma – actions that must have effects. But as each of these fails to become a fresh cause, the burden of karma is reduced; and when it is reduced to zero, the Gita says, there is nothing to compel action; we act and live in freedom:

> They live in freedom who have gone beyond the dualities of life. Competing with no one, they are alike in success and failure and content with whatever comes to them. They are free, without selfish attachments; their minds are fixed in knowledge. They perform all work in the spirit of service, and their karma is dissolved.
> (4:22–23)

Karma yoga is praised throughout the Gita; since all of us must act in one way or another, Sri Krishna says, we should learn how to act selflessly because that alone will help us free ourselves from the results of past karma. But you can see why a true karma yogi is so rare. The best example I can point to in our own times who embodies this path is Mahatma Gandhi, and he is quite candid about how difficult he found it to work tirelessly for others without getting attached to things turning out his way.

The key to this is given in some of the most famous verses in the Gita:

> You have the right to work, but never to the fruit of work. You should never engage in action for the sake of reward, nor should you long for inaction. Perform work in this world, Arjuna, as a man established within himself – without selfish attachments, and alike in success and defeat. For yoga is perfect evenness of mind. (2:47–48)

This sounds prescriptive, but Sri Krishna is just pointing out something we all know but can't easily accept: we have really no control over the results of what we do. Even with something that seems completely within our domain, a million things can go wrong; a million events can change the outcome in an instant. We can't control the universe; we are doing well if we manage to control ourselves. Therefore, Sri Krishna says, it is within our power to act wisely, but wise not to be anxious about getting what we want. Gandhi summarized this in a memorable aphorism: "Do your best, then leave the results to God."

Krishna goes on to explain the value of this kind of detachment:

Those who are motivated only by desire for the fruits of
action are miserable, for they are constantly anxious
about the results of what they do. When consciousness
is unified, however, all vain anxiety is left behind. There
is no cause for worry, whether things go well or ill.
Therefore, devote yourself to the disciplines of yoga, for
yoga is skill in action. (2:49–50)

In practical terms, he is reminding us that worry, vacillation, and other divisions in consciousness only weaken our
resolve and disturb our focus. When Mahatma Gandhi had
to make a decision, he would put his attention on the problem completely, work out the pros and cons, and listen to
trusted advice before deciding what to do. Then, once he had
made his decision, he didn't pay the slightest attention to praise
or blame or even threats. It's not that he ignored the outcome;
when he decided he had miscalculated, he could reverse himself spectacularly. But he was always in the driver's seat, not
pushed and pulled about by what other people thought.

The result of this is just marvelous: you don't lose your nerve
when things go wrong. The main reason why we get afraid of
obstacles and anxious about problems, the Gita says, is that we
become entangled in getting the results we want. The secret of
karma yoga lies in using right means to achieve a right end, and
then not getting anxious over the outcome. When we have
learned to drop attachment to getting what we want while working hard and selflessly for a great cause, we can work without

anxiety, with confidence and peace of mind. Reverses will come, but they will only drive us deeper into our consciousness.

> Better indeed is knowledge than mechanical practice.
> Better than knowledge is meditation. But better still is
> surrender of attachment to results, because there fol-
> lows immediate peace. (12:12)

As I said earlier, this is a very tall order. One could practice it for a lifetime and still feel a beginner, as Gandhi said. Nevertheless, it is important for every one of us to do our best to learn this skill in every aspect of our lives, because the need for selfless service has become so urgent. We live in a world of immense turbulence. You have only to pick up a newspaper to see that none of us can afford to chase after personal profit or pleasure while the world seethes with problems which globalization brings right to our front door.

According to the Gita, we have been sent into the world to grapple with these problems: to sow love where there is hatred, pardon where there is injury, joy where there is sadness, light where there is darkness. This is what we are born for, and when we pursue private desires instead, the Gita reminds us that we are using time that has been granted to us for contributing to the welfare of others rather than ourselves:

> Anyone who enjoys the things given by the devas with-
> out offering selfless acts in return is a thief. (3:12)

In this connection, it is an important part of karma yoga to make sure that our occupation is not at the expense of others. Making money from products or activities that are harmful, such as cigarettes or weapons, sets a low ceiling on spiritual growth. This is a personal decision that will change as understanding deepens, but it is helpful to remember that in the Gita's view, the goal of all work is spiritual wisdom.

Bhakti Yoga

The third path is bhakti yoga, the way of love or devotion, which is ideally suited to the modern world because it is natural to forget ourselves for those we love. This precious capacity is part of being human; we see it whenever a mother stays up all night caring for her sick baby or when husband or wife deny themselves something for the sake of the family. In each such instance, we forget ourselves a little in the interests of others; separateness is dissolved a bit, if only for a while, in something greater than ourselves. Bhakti yoga consists in extending such moments until we forget ourselves completely in the welfare of all – in which, we must remember, our own happiness and welfare are included.

Love is one of the most misused words in the English language. We use it so indiscriminately! We say we love chocolate, we love TV, we love Paris in the spring . . . If we want to talk about love as a path to the supreme reality, we have first to dispel the absurd idea that love has anything to do with the body or senses. Nor has it really anything to do with the mind: love is not an emotion but a state of consciousness. We have to learn to love, and that requires a tremendous amount of effort because love is the precise opposite of self-will. As we have seen, in most personal relationships there is a tendency to mold the other person in one's own image, which closes the door to love. Where there is self-will, love simply cannot last. There will always be attempts to use the other person, however unwittingly, and great agitation when the other person doesn't bend to this use.

The Sanskrit word *bhakti* means a state of consciousness in which you forget yourself. Bhakti yoga is the art of extending this from one relationship ultimately to all of life. There are examples of this kind of love in all the world's great traditions; I think immediately of Francis of Assisi in the West and Meera in India. The best embodiment of the path of love in my personal experience is my own spiritual teacher, my grandmother, who showed that it is possible to learn to forget oneself completely in the welfare of those around.

The Yoga of the Bhagavad Gita

It is customary to view these three paths as alternatives, and throughout the Gita Sri Krishna does seem to recommend one over others. What confuses Arjuna – and us – is that his recommendations vary:

> O Krishna, your advice seems inconsistent. Give me
> one path to follow to the supreme good. (3:2)

Yet Krishna is always replying in context in response to a particular question. His answers are relative rather than absolute. Most important, they are not exclusive. The natural way to approach the Gita is to take it whole and follow a way of life in which these three paths are combined. That is what I have done in my own life, and when this is done, it is clear that these three yogas complement each other and ultimately blend into one.

This approach is particularly effective in today's fast-paced, media-saturated way of life. When Arjuna asks, "Which is the better path, jnana or bhakti?" we have to ask the question for ourselves today and not as it was asked thousands of years ago. We are not hermits or ascetics; we live in a very different world, about as far removed from a natural way of life as one can imagine: a world based on the conviction that we are separate, physical creatures whose job in life is to look out for number one. We must take into account what is called the *yuga dharma*, the dharma of the times – its needs, its background, its capacities, its problems – which means that wisdom, love, and selfless service are essential for everyone.

How to integrate these three into daily life, however, is far from obvious. We need a many-faceted approach that includes jnana yoga and karma yoga, both led harmoniously by bhakti yoga and all three based on what the Gita calls dhyana yoga, the practice of meditation. Without the regular, sincere, systematic practice of meditation, I don't think it is possible for most of us in the modern world to develop spiritual wisdom, engage in truly selfless action, or forget ourselves in the love of God in all. The layers of physical conditioning today are simply too thick. We need some way to drill into deeper levels, below the surface of consciousness, and that is just where meditation excels:

> Meditation is superior to asceticism and the path of
> knowledge. It is also superior to selfless service. May
> you attain the goal of meditation, Arjuna! (6:46)

⬥ *Wisdom Through Meditation*

MEDITATION IS TRAINING the mind: teaching attention to stay on a single focus until the mind becomes as concentrated as a laser, able to penetrate deep into consciousness without effort.

> Closing their eyes, steadying their breathing, and
> focusing their attention on the center of spiritual con-
> sciousness, the wise master their senses, mind, and
> intellect through meditation. Self-realization is their
> only goal. Freed from selfish desire, fear, and anger,
> they live in freedom always. (5:27–28)

This kind of absorption is not as alien as it may sound. All of us get absorbed in a hobby or activity we enjoy greatly – so absorbed that we don't hear the cars outside or the dog bark-ing or a call to dinner; we forget financial and family prob-lems; we may even forget our body and our surroundings. At such times we are completely happy, though we may be aware of it only afterwards.

Again, everybody gets concentrated when going through an emotional upheaval. That's why we can't attend to things outside very easily, can't pay attention to other people. That is what concentration does when it is compulsive.

These are important clues. The reason we are happy, the Gita would say, is that we have forgotten ourselves – if only for a short time, while we hold the outside world at bay. And the reason we are miserable in an emotional crisis is that we can't get our attention off ourselves; all we can think about is our problems. What we do in meditation is free attention from all conditioning so that we can direct it where we choose, and then turn it inwards so that instead of getting absorbed in what we like or caught in what we dislike, we lead attention deeper and deeper until it becomes absorbed in the Self:

> Little by little, through patience and repeated effort, the mind will become stilled in the Self. Wherever the mind wanders, restless and diffuse in its search for satisfaction without, lead it within; train it to rest in the Self. (6:25–26)

Until we learn this art, however, the problem with attention is that we have virtually no control over it. The mind is like a television set that does whatever it wants. We are compelled to watch what it puts before us; it chooses its own channels and virtually never turns itself off. And we say, "Isn't that wonderful? Our TV is spontaneous. Why should we try to control it?"

Mastering the mind is an adventure that should appeal to anyone with daring who wants to make a contribution to life. Meditation is an extremely difficult discipline; it cannot be mastered easily or in a short time. How many years does it take to become a world-class athlete or pianist or ballerina? It is the same story with meditation: it calls for sustained enthusiasm, unflagging initiative, and the capacity to keep meeting higher challenges with greater endurance.

To illustrate with a bit of science fiction, I have read that when Einstein was a boy, he wanted to ride on a wave of light. I've always enjoyed the thought of little Albert straddling a beam of light as if it were a Harley-Davidson, racing along at a hundred and eighty-six thousand miles a second. Similarly, we can imagine meditation as riding on a wave of thought from the surface level of awareness right through the preconscious and the personal unconscious and then breaking into the collective unconscious, leaping chasm after chasm until coming to rest on the very seabed of the unconscious with the mind completely still. But this isn't really science fiction. It has been done, and the adventure is timeless, open to everyone today as it was thousands of years ago.

No adventure worth the name is without dangers, and meditation is no exception. I used to say this right at the outset when teaching meditation on the Berkeley campus. One student who had all the requisite daring came and asked if he could attend my class. I had heard reports about him from his friends, so I warned him, "Yes, you will be able to learn to meditate. But I don't think you will be able to stay with it." I knew the division in his consciousness. When he reached a critical juncture in meditation and had to choose whether to resist his problems or hold on to them, he stopped meditating and left town.

These disciplines may be simple, but they are terribly powerful, and they assume a simple way of life in a pure environment that is very, very far from how we live today. I hadn't encountered problems with this until I came to the United States, when I met two or three people who had been experimenting with occult breathing exercises and managed to split their personalities into two.

One of these men came to me for help, and it was like talking to two different people: one part of his mind would be in charge while I was telling him things; then another part of the mind would take over and he would give me a completely different response. After a while I managed to discover what he had been doing and was able to get him out of it – a real tribute to the resilience of the human system. For me it was a study in the enormous risks of so-called spiritual practices when undertaken without an experienced guide.

One more requisite for meditation should be mentioned:

determination. St. Teresa put this right at the top of her list, and Sri Ramana Maharshi was partial to his British disciples because of what he called their bulldog resolve to stick it out whatever happens.

Soon after I came to this country, an international team of mountain climbers set out to scale Mount Everest. As differences emerged, people from various countries started falling out with each other, and one by one they withdrew from the expedition before they were halfway up. The only two who stayed on were the British. This is the spirit that is required in meditation too, not for conquering mountains but for mastering the mind.

> The supreme reality stands revealed in the consciousness of those who have conquered themselves. They live in peace, alike in cold and heat, pleasure and pain, praise and blame. . . . Having conquered their senses, they have climbed to the summit of human consciousness. To such people a clod of dirt, a stone, and gold are the same. They are equally disposed to family, enemies, and friends, to those who support them and those who are hostile, to the good and the evil alike. (6:7–9)

The purpose of meditation is to make the mind what the Gita calls "one-pointed": completely focused on a single point. Most of us have grasshopper minds, constantly jumping from subject to subject, from worry to worry, from fear to fear.

That's the nature of the mind. Our job is to teach attention to remain on a single focus, not in the world outside but within consciousness, which will "lead it to dwell on the Self":

> Those who aspire to the state of yoga should seek the Self in inner solitude through meditation. With body and mind controlled they should constantly practice one-pointedness, free from expectations and attachment to material possessions. (6:10)

Verse after verse like this tells us that meditation by itself is not enough. We can't train attention in meditation and then let the mind do as it likes the rest of the day. Imagine training a puppy that way! Training the mind is an all-day job, and all classical methods of meditation are part of a set of supportive disciplines – in Sanskrit, *sadhana* – to be followed during the day.

These disciplines are universal: in addition to meditation, they include keeping the mind one-pointed, reading the scriptures, protecting the senses from unnecessary stimulation, reducing self-will, voluntary simplicity, and selfless service. The program I follow has eight such points; it is essentially based on the regular practice of meditation and expresses itself in selfless service.

You may remember my saying earlier that the movement of the mind *is* the mind. When the mind stays on a single focus and does not wander, so that the flow of attention is as smooth and unbroken as oil poured from one vessel into another, the activity of the mind quietly dissolves and the mind becomes still, as limpid and transparent as the still waters of a crystal-clear lake. This is the goal of meditation:

> Select a clean spot, neither too high nor too low, and seat yourself firmly on a cloth, a deerskin, and kusha grass. Then, once seated, strive to still your thoughts. Make your mind one-pointed in meditation, and your heart will be purified.
>
> Hold your body, head, and neck firmly in a straight line, and keep your eyes from wandering. With all fears dissolved in the peace of the Self and all actions dedicated to Brahman, controlling the mind and fixing it on me, sit in meditation with me as your only goal.
>
> With senses and mind constantly controlled through meditation, united with the Self within, an aspirant attains nirvana, the state of abiding joy and peace in me.
>
> Through constant effort, aspirants learn to withdraw the mind from selfish cravings and absorb it in the Self. Thus they attain the state of yoga. (6:11–15, 18)

It is significant that here (and elsewhere) the Gita uses the same word that the Buddha chose: *nirvana,* literally the blowing-out or extinction of all self-centered thought. I like to put this positively: it is in forgetting our small self that we awaken to our real Self, in which we and others are one.

The method of meditation I follow is inspired by the passage from the Bhagavad Gita that I just quoted. I will draw my illustrations from this method since it is the one I know and teach, but these comments should apply equally well to any other classical method that follows the Gita's guidelines. My approach uses universal passages from the scriptures or the world's great mystics as a focus, rather than something external, so that attention is drawn deep inwards, away from the world of the senses.

To be appropriate for meditation, such passages should be positive, practical, inspiring, and universal. And they should express our highest ideals, because we become what we meditate on. My own first choices were from the Gita, but wisdom is universal, and I have found it helpful to have a repertoire of passages with universal appeal drawn from all the great religions. Meditation is a skill, not a ritual; it belongs to no religion and has nothing to do with doctrines or metaphysics or theology.

Meditation involves sitting quietly while keeping attention on your chosen focus and not letting it wander. In the method I follow, this means going slowly through the words of a passage such as the second chapter of the Gita, trying to give full attention to each word or phrase. Whenever the mind wanders, bring it gently back:

Wherever the mind wanders, restless and diffuse in its
search for satisfaction without, lead it within; train it
to rest in the Self. Abiding joy comes to those who still
the mind. Freeing themselves from the taint of self-will,
with their consciousness unified, they become one with
Brahman. (6:26–27)

For a long time, it is inevitable that distractions will come
in; that is the nature of the mind. It has got to keep moving,
from thought to thought, from desire to desire, from feeling
to feeling, from memory to memory; that is simply the way it
works. We are trying to teach it to stay put, but the problem is
that resisting distractions like these as they arise simply gives
them more attention and makes them stronger. A more effective strategy is simple: instead of resisting distractions, just
give more attention to what you are meditating on. It is almost
like training a dog: you bring it back, calmly and patiently,
until it learns.

Actually, in meditation, any kind of discursive thinking is
a distraction. No matter what the mind turns to, it is not stay-
ing where we put it; it is doing what it wants instead. We call
this thinking, but most of the time it is just yak-yak-yakking,
the mind talking to itself. As your mind becomes one-
pointed, you will find this kind of thing quite bothersome.
For me, this has gone to such an extent that when I go to the
movie theater, I like to sit far away from people who bring in

those big tubs of popcorn; it reminds me of the mind, munching, munching, munching all the time.

We had a woman in our village who had a genius for discursive thinking. She would talk without a break, jumping from one subject to another almost sentence by sentence – a hundred subjects in the course of one hour. She would ask my mother, "Do you know what happened to Raman?" and by the time my mother could say, "No, what?" she would be talking about Shankaran instead. It was an extreme case of a grasshopper mind. In most of us this is not so obvious because it doesn't spill over into speech, but once we start meditating and glimpse what the mind is really up to, we are likely to discover that our thoughts too are jumping all over the place.

In meditation, therefore, whenever your mind wanders away – to the movie theater or the swimming pool or the restaurant or the boutique – don't get angry; just tap your mind on the shoulder and say, "Please come back." Every time. It's a dull, difficult discipline. The mind may wander thirty times in thirty minutes – a very conservative estimate. But even a little practice of this during meditation brings immediate benefits during the rest of the day. Many problems that we take for granted are not really necessary; they arise from attention getting distracted and caught without our consent. For example, all of us are familiar with the toll negative memories can take. When they come up, they simply won't let us alone.

They claim our attention, and dwelling on them only makes them stronger. The mind gets upset until finally the body begins to suffer. But if you can turn attention away, just as you do in meditation, the memory will gradually lose its emotional charge. The memory itself is not lost; it simply loses its compulsive hold on you.

Again, when a friend has offended you, it is not your friend that causes the agitation; it is dwelling on what happened. Attention is caught, and the mind cannot stop thinking about it. When you go to the theater, you can't pay attention to the film. When you go to bed, you can't stop thinking about what happened, so you toss and turn all night. Dwelling on resentment or hostility or any other negative emotion magnifies it; the answer is to turn attention away.

One benefit of this deserves special mention. I said earlier that happiness comes when we forget ourselves, and misery when we can't think about anybody else. This is essentially a problem of attention getting trapped. One of the greatest benefits of meditation is that it releases the precious faculty of redirecting our love and attention from our little selves so it can flow towards other people. It's an exhilarating experience, because most of us have no idea the capacity for love we have imprisoned.

You can get a glimpse of how powerful a distracted mind can be by seeing how it can affect others. Haven't you seen people who, when something happens to them, take it out on their partner, their children, their colleagues, even their dog? All right, the Gita would say, you had a mishap, but confine it to your own lane. Why weave off into other people's lanes and cause collisions there too?

When I am out on the freeway, I sometimes see a driver weaving all over the road. The mind drives like that, darting from lane to lane for no apparent reason. In meditation, when you start to see what the mind does when it thinks no one is looking, it's almost like watching one of those Hollywood chase scenes where cars careen through traffic at breakneck speed until they jump off the road and crash into a tree. Why should we let ourselves be driven about like that? Meditation is getting behind the wheel and getting the mind under control. At first we may not be able to stay in the same lane all the time; we still get angry or afraid. But instead of getting really angry, we'll get half angry – instead of throwing things, we'll be able to take them up, make a gesture, and then put them down. It's a beginning. Gradually we reach the point where the mind is tuned like a Ferrari and completely under our control. Then we set out for our destination and cruise along in one lane – unbroken, effortless concentration. Distractions may be weaving about, trying to get our attention, but that doesn't mean we have to look.

Sometimes, even in the early years, waves of emotion can sweep over us in meditation. This too is a distraction: not always negative, but a distraction nevertheless. We are letting the mind grab the wheel. The emotion might be fear; it might be a profound catharsis that brings a flood of tears. At other times a great wave of love or gratitude may threaten to overwhelm us. Whatever comes, that is the time to concentrate more and not pay attention to the emotion by trying to analyze it or bask in it, which Catherine of Siena compares with a bee caught in its own honey. When we are able to concentrate even more on the passage during a wave of emotion, concentration is strengthened enormously, bringing great benefits during the rest of the day – and protecting us from the inevitable emotional plunge when the mind swings the other way.

Training the mind like this in meditation calls for immense patience, but with practice, the great day will come when the mind does not wander at all. Then you will be able to give complete attention to anything you choose, which is the mark of genius in any field. Not only that, it is the secret of effective work and lasting personal relationships. With people, at work, everywhere, by not letting the mind get pulled and pushed about by circumstances, you are making yourself unshakable – less and less fickle, and therefore more and more real, because what is real never changes. When concentration is complete like this, personal sorrow comes to an end:

But when you move amidst the world of sense, free
from attachment and aversion alike, there comes the

peace in which all sorrows end, and you live in the wisdom of the Self. (2:64–65)

Distractions often seem small, but they pack tremendous power. All that energy is consolidated and harnessed as the mind becomes one-pointed. To get a sense of what power the mind has, when you have a powerful sexual desire, just try to sit down and write an essay on the benefits of yoga. The same test is equally effective with anger or fear. If you find it difficult to control a strong sexual drive even for a minute, imagine the power that can flow into your hands as your meditation deepens.

It takes a while, of course, even to get below the surface of consciousness in meditation. One of the surest signs that this is happening is a confidence that your life is coming under your control, that circumstances can no longer hold you hostage. This brings a wave of hope which time and practice will turn to certitude. It is not that you expect life to go your way, but you know that in some deep sense, as Julian of Norwich said beautifully, "All shall be well. All manner of thing shall be well."

Yet challenges do come. When you reach a certain level in meditation, for example, there is a real danger that you will encourage your mind to wander. Sri Ramakrishna, comparing meditation with flying a kite, calls this letting go of the string, which can happen when we come across something in consciousness that we don't want to face.

For some people, the easiest way of resisting going deeper in meditation is simply to fall asleep. Others get so restless in meditation that even if mentally they are making a good effort, physically all that effort is neutralized. If you are able to keep your body reasonably still for half an hour of meditation, it's a good sign that the mind is becoming still as well, which means that meditation is deepening.

After some years of practice, when you have been making good progress, you reach the top of a peak thinking that you have reached the goal and everything is finished. Then you look and see an abyss, beyond which rises an even higher peak. Now how do you proceed? There is no path, not even any ground to walk on; there is nothing you can do. Eventually there is no choice but to leap, and however brave you may be, if there is a fear lurking in your mind at that time, consciousness will split and you won't be able to make it. Fortunately, simply reaching this point means that you do have the capacity to make the leap. But faith is required – one reason why deeper meditation should never be tackled without an experienced teacher, a point emphasized in our Hindu scriptures.

In the early stages of meditation, concentration requires effort because so much attention is still on the activities of the day. You have got to sweep all that under the rug and then put the broom away, which takes a bit of time. Eventually, however, as your desires get completely unified, you reach a stage where no more effort is necessary. I don't know how to explain that; you can call it effortless effort. It isn't even concentration; it has gone beyond concentration because you are not really there. Attention is unbroken, which means there is really no movement at all:

> When meditation is mastered, the mind is unwavering
> like the flame of a lamp in a windless place. In the still
> mind, in the depths of meditation, the Self reveals itself.
> (6:19–20)

It's beautiful poetry. Look at the flame of a candle unruffled by the slightest movement of air; it will burn like a hot gem.

At this point, with concentration one-pointed, the mind is almost completely still. Some kind of whispering does go on in the corners of consciousness, but the chattering that passed for thinking has grown quiet. This brings such profound peace in your heart that it spreads to everyone around you. The highest happiness comes to you – happiness that cannot be captured; it comes to you unbidden. With no agitation in your mind, you are always able to give. And there is a loveliness about your life, your face, your eyes, all reflecting the peace in the depths of consciousness.

At this depth in meditation, your mind is so concentrated that there is hardly any movement. Instead of chatter, wisdom wells up that needs no words. There is no compulsion, no conditioning, just a continuous stream of pure awareness. All consciousness has been withdrawn from the senses into the mind, so the eyes and ears don't register; the sensory world has been left behind. In that state, as I said earlier, if you cannot observe yourself through your senses, you – the observer – don't really have a body. Then observer and observed are one. You are at the level of pure energy, the same energy that flows through all of life, untouched by time, by age, by death. It is by repeating this experience over and over again that you come to realize the words of the Gita:

> You were never born; you will never die. You have never
> changed; you can never change. Unborn, eternal,
> immutable, immemorial, you do not die when the body
> dies. (2:20)

Once you realize this truth, the Gita says, there is nothing more the world can offer. You cannot be shaken by the heaviest burden of sorrow. This is yoga, which breaks the connection with suffering.

Perhaps the most amazing development in the final stages of meditation is the disappearance of the barrier between the world within and the world without, which means the barrier between yourself and others has fallen. Once that barrier falls, how can you be jealous? How can you be afraid? How can you be angry? In the language of the Gita, you will be seeing everyone in yourself and seeing yourself in all, which is the consummation of unconditioned love:

> They see the Self in every creature and all creation in the Self. With consciousness unified through meditation, they see everything with an equal eye.
>
> I am ever present to those who have realized me in every creature. Seeing all life as my manifestation, they are never separated from me. They worship me in the hearts of all, and all their actions proceed from me. Wherever they may live, they abide in me. Responding to the joys and sorrows of others as if they were their own, they have attained perfection in yoga. (6:29–32)

Ultimately, even the smallest of distractions in meditation arises from the very split in consciousness that we are trying to heal. Most attempts to heal this split are like putting a Band-Aid over it and saying you are healed, you are whole: the split is still there, just hidden. Yoga may take years to reach its goal, but it brings complete healing, from the surface of consciousness to the bottom: that is, from everyday behavior to the very depths of the unconscious. How this happens is the subject of the next two chapters.

◇ *Yoga as Skill in Daily Living*

ONE OF THE characteristic contributions of the Bhagavad Gita is its emphasis on life as a duality. Pleasure and pain, heat and cold, honor and dishonor, profit and loss, friend and foe – paired phrases like these, in the Gita's usage, are shorthand for the position that life as we experience it is always an encounter with opposites. However much we might wish this were otherwise – and always wishing it to be otherwise seems part of our mental makeup – no one has ever succeeded in isolating pleasure and avoiding pain, in winning respect without incurring disapproval, or generally getting anything the way one wants in any aspect of life at all. It simply is not possible; that's not how life is.

Of course, we all know this, but that doesn't stop the mind from incessantly wishing that things were different – which, as my grandmother liked to say, is like asking a banana tree to give you mangoes.

However, the Gita isn't talking about being realistic about

what we want. It is making a point that is absolutely central to understanding how to live. The duality of life as we experience it is not a feature of life as it is; it is imposed by the makeup of the mind itself. It is an upadhi, an apparent limitation imposed on reality by each level of the mind.

In fact, at one of these levels – that of buddhi, the intellect or higher mind – defining opposites is the basic function. Its very purpose is to make distinctions, so that we can decide what is beneficial and what is not, what is true and what is false, and so forth. We would be well enough off if things stopped there, but they do not. The lower mind steps in to insist on what it desires, which of course is often opposed to the higher judgment about what is beneficial; and the stickier our attachment to getting what we want, the more likely it is that the higher mind is going to get overruled. At the physical level, the body and senses join the discussion with their own insistence on getting what is pleasing. And at the root, as usual, is the ego, with its division between itself and the rest of life.

This makes life a roller-coaster ride. The mind is constantly up, down, or wobbling, depending on how much we like or dislike what the world is giving us at the moment. Happiness will come our way today, sorrow will come tomorrow, and we get elated when happiness comes and downhearted when sorrow follows. Similarly, as long as we are susceptible to adulation, we are going to be susceptible to censure; as long as we get elated by success, we will get depressed by failure.

We will be happy when people like us and unhappy when we think they don't. This is the practical meaning of that abstract idea about a split in consciousness: it drives the mind to constant turmoil and vacillation.

And the Gita, of course, is telling us that we don't have to live this way. We can't stop life from going up and down, but we don't have to go up and down with it. Instead of wishing the world would give us what we want, we can, through the disciplines of yoga, go beyond the duality of a divided mind. And when we do, we find that instead of liking this and disliking that, we live continuously in a higher state that the Upanishads call *ananda:* joy. Liking and disliking are emotions, pleasure and pain are sensations; all these belong to the phenomenal world. Joy is a state of consciousness, on a different level altogether.

The Indian scriptures illustrate this with a beautiful image. In a tropical country the weather can be quite dramatic, particularly during a monsoon storm. You can watch masses of indigo-blue rainclouds gather at the horizon and sweep towards you minute by minute till they cover the sky, so you can see neither the sun during the day nor moon and stars at night. But the sky itself is unaffected. When black clouds come, the sky doesn't curl up and hide; it's not even touched, and we know it's only a matter of time before the clouds are swept away. Similarly, the scriptures say, when thoughts flit across the mind, they needn't affect us. Even disturbing thoughts such as anger or fear, which come to all of us, are no more than clouds that darken the mind as they pass.

In practice, this means that when negative thoughts come, we can try to behave as if we are not influenced by them. For example, even if you don't like somebody, try to behave as if you do by talking to him with respect and listening to his point of view. All you have to do is not act on what you feel. Don't use harsh words, don't walk out, don't refuse to cooperate. Every time you try this, it brings more detachment. It *is* difficult; no one has ever called it easy. But if you can practice this systematically, day by day, most of the agitation in the mind will stop, which means there is no wear and tear on the nervous system.

Of course, the comment this immediately provokes is, "Isn't this utterly hypocritical? Does the Gita want us to pretend?" Not at all. This is our real nature; it is anger that is hypocrisy. Even if kindness seems a pretense, it is being true to our real Self. All things considered, given that we are dealing with many years of conditioning to the contrary, it is remarkable how quickly we come to understand that this *is* our real nature. This can happen almost miraculously when consciousness is unified, as Sri Krishna promises in verses that have consoled millions:

> Whatever you do, make it an offering to me – the food you eat, the sacrifices you make, the help you give, even your suffering. . . .

Even sinners become holy when they take refuge in me
alone. Quickly their souls conform to dharma and they
attain to boundless peace. Never forget this, Arjuna: no
one who is devoted to me will ever come to harm.
(9:27, 30–31)

To practice this, it is helpful to think of ourselves as actors
learning a role. I discovered this when I was a professor in
India just learning to meditate. When I started climbing the
academic ladder, on the first day I had to lecture in class I
wanted to produce a good impression. I imagined my students going home and telling their parents, "He is *it*!" Unfortunately, I don't think I succeeded in producing that impression. I was too attached to what my students would think of
me, so I couldn't really give my best.

As I began to practice meditation, however, I realized that I
was not really a fledgling professor; I was the Self, and had no
need to woo the opinion of students because the Self is complete. Gradually this brought some detachment, so that when
I had difficult students, I found I could move closer to them.
The more detached I became, the easier it was to identify
myself with my students and understand their needs. Instead
of dwelling upon myself and getting caught up in other people's opinions, I could concentrate on doing a good job.

Of course, this was difficult. Every day brought problems, not only from students but from other faculty members, the financial committee, even the janitor. But I kept

concentrating on doing my best – and then, when I left campus for the day, I dropped that role like a cloak, so that I didn't take those problems home with me; I left them on my desk. "All the world's a stage," I used to remind myself, "and professors and students merely players."

As your mind becomes more even, less susceptible to ups and downs, you will find it easier to distinguish between a person and a point of view. To most of us, the person *is* the point of view – or, perhaps, the point of view is the person. We identify people with their politics or their opinion of other generations or even their preferences in what they wear, and of course with their outbursts of temper or the difficulties we think they cause. When we think, "She was so harsh to me," we are identifying that person with these words. Actually, the Gita would say, there is no connection between that person and that particular outburst. There is no more basis for identifying people with their opinions than for identifying them with the colors they wear. When we are able to distinguish between a person and his opinions, we begin to see the unity of life: not only with individuals, but with countries, cultures, and races as well.

"Wait," we want to protest. "Isn't this a counsel of perfection?" Perhaps, but even if perfection is beyond our reach, that does not mean we should fail to reach for it. In fact, the Gita would say we should all be perfectionists because the seed of perfection is within us. Compared to the exhilarating creativity of cultivating this seed into full bloom, I think the satisfaction even of practicing the fine arts is negligible – and I say this after nearly half a lifetime of immersion in poetry, fiction, and classical music and dance. The pursuit of perfection in one's own life is simply on another level: life is a much richer medium than any art at its disposal. In that sense I would say that Mahatma Gandhi and Francis of Assisi were great artists, working on their lives every minute.

In whatever walk of life we may be engaged, once we take to meditation, life becomes vibrant with meaning because every moment we have a choice – if you like, between immediate personal gratification and personal growth, between personal desires and the welfare of all. It is this exercise of choice that slowly begins to transform all that is ugly in our life and consciousness into a work of art.

According to the Gita, each of us can develop the capacity to unbuild the edifice of personality that has been built under the pressure of personal pleasure and profit and then rebuild it brick by brick in the image of the perfection placed before us by our real nature. Whatever mistakes we may have committed, whatever faults we feel burdened by, in our heart of hearts we are one hundred percent pure, one hundred percent perfect. Gradually, we can identify ourselves completely with this purity and perfection that is the Atman, the Self within.

Until we try it out, we cannot understand what joy there

is in this. Even though in the early days it may not be very pleasant – in fact, we may positively dislike doing what we are doing – over a longer period, life becomes joyful and free. It is when we get caught in things we like that we make ourselves rigid; it is a grand experience to be elastic and flexible whatever life brings. Then we are never forced into the position "I don't like this, so I will not do it; I like this, so I will." In the language of the Gita, this is bondage; the goal of yoga is freedom.

When the mind is even, we can be comfortable everywhere. The Gita's language is quite homey: *prasanna cetasa.* The mind is cheerful always, so cheerful that it almost smiles. Many of us, however, have a self-willed streak in consciousness that isolates us from others and prompts a nagging sense of not being at home anywhere, of not belonging. Wherever we go, we are uncomfortable; we travel in a cage of insecurity. The problem lies in the state of consciousness, so that is where the correction has to be made. Changing to a deeper level of consciousness brings an increasing sense of unity that makes us comfortable with everybody.

A young friend recalling her university days once told me that when she arrived in New York, she lived at first in what she called "rather ratty digs." I had the impression that "ratty" was more than metaphorical. She didn't waste time trying to patch up the place; she simply moved on as soon as she could find somewhere better. It is the same in meditation. You may remember my saying earlier that in meditation, instead of trying to fix problems one by one, we go to the root: the mind. What this means is that we gradually move to a deeper level of consciousness, and when we do, we see that the problems belonging to the previous level have simply been left behind. Instead of trying to fix up the tenement of the mind, we just move on to a place where we can feel more at home.

To cultivate a sense of kinship with others, of course, we need to *be* with others, work together with others, to rub off the angles and corners of personality. Many people have difficulty in building satisfactory personal relationships, primarily because they haven't learned this skill. If one word is said that they don't like, they get agitated; if one act is done that they do not like, they get agitated. If they do not get their way, they get agitated; if others get *their* way, they get agitated. All this can be set right through the simple practice of learning to be more patient.

The Gita praises patience the way Linus Pauling praised vitamin C. "Emotional flu is coming, bad-relationships flu is coming, insecurity flu is coming; start inoculating yourself now with vitamin P. You don't have to go queue up in line, don't have to feel the prick of the needle, don't have to get fever for twenty-four hours, don't have to go around with an aching arm; you can do this right where you are."

Sometimes, of course, no patience is required of us. People are nice – that is, they agree exactly with what we say. But sometimes they are not very nice. They don't want to follow our way of thinking: they have their own way – and that's what upsets us. When the mind has been conditioned to separateness, there's a little voice that whispers, "Quit. Run." All you want to do is to rush out, jump on your Honda, and blaze off into the sunset. That's the time when you stay in your chair, plant your feet on the ground, and stick it out. Don't leave the room and walk out; that is running away from the battle. It's a simple suggestion: not to move away from people who upset you, because this is how we learn to make the mind un-upsettable.

And that's the challenge. You not only stay where you are; you move closer. Your body may flinch, but you sit down patiently and listen with attention – perhaps to things that set your teeth on edge. Then, if necessary, you state your own views with quiet detachment and complete respect. This requires a lot of practice, and for a long time there will be some people with whom the best you can do is to stay out of their way and avoid confrontation and deprecation. As with learning any skill, you can expect mistakes. But this is the kind of practice that is necessary to feel comfortable with everybody, and even a little of it pays off handsomely.

It follows that by dropping out of life, avoiding people, playing the lone wolf, we actually forfeit the opportunity to grow. I have met a few people who have a gift for isolating themselves like this; wherever they go, they build a wall around themselves. My heart goes out to such people because they are self-made prisoners, for whom even a little release is painfully difficult. Even if you have trouble with those you are living with, Sri Krishna would say, it's much better to live with them and learn to resolve quarrels than to move away. Look upon it as an opportunity to learn the give and take of life.

When Christine and I were in India in the sixties, we met one solitary Hindu hippie. He was an unusual person, quite sensitive, but he had dropped out of life. He had become so much a prisoner of himself that we could hardly understand his conversation; he hadn't talked to people for so long that his voice was almost inaudible. When we met him he had wandered up to the Blue Mountain, where he spent about a year near where we lived. Gradually he began to feel closer to us, so we saw him more and more often. He used to think I was too fond of people and tried to tempt me to walk with him into the mountains or forests. I would protest, "We're already in the mountains! I like mountains and forests and rivers, but it's people that I love. I like being with people all the time, and if I can't get peaceful people, I would rather be with troubled people." He began to think that there was something lacking in my character.

Then one day, at the ashram where we were conducting the meditation, he had to work shoulder to shoulder with another young man who was hot-tempered. They traded some unkind remarks, and this Hindu hippie, who prided himself on being nonviolent, took a spade and was about to fight. He came to see me in the evening and I said teasingly, "You're not a hippie. Where is your flower power? This is all fist power."

He got quite ashamed. "How is it," he asked, "that I don't know how to deal with this? How can I get so angry?"

I told him, "This is what you learn by living with people. Everyone gets angry sometimes, but you have run away from your family and community; you don't have the facilities for training. It *is* difficult to live with others, but that's the only way to learn."

I could sympathize with this question, though. It's a universal question; even Arjuna asks, "What makes me do these things, Krishna? As if compelled to, against my will?" It's an inability we can all confess to. Sri Krishna will give a detailed answer, but the gist of it is simple: Change your consciousness not to change. That is the secret. When consciousness does not change, does not vacillate, we can be the same person always.

This is what we try to do in meditation. When you keep bringing attention back every time it wanders, what you are learning is to keep your mind from going up and down. For most of us, the mind goes up and down most of the day. Sometimes we are up, sometimes we are down; sometimes we are high, sometimes we are low; and each time we see the world differently, so we relate differently to other people. When consciousness is unitary, we can relate the same way every day, everywhere, to everybody.

Yet as we have seen, there is resistance to this at every level of personality. Each has its own variety of sticky attachments. Imagine those Russian dolls being glued together, each with its own kind of glue! On the physical level, we know how easy it is to get caught in attachment to pleasures and possessions. The emotional level brings crippling dependencies on other people – and, worst, attachment to ourselves. Even the higher mind gets involved when we get fiercely attached to personal opinions. And deepest of all is the ego, where all these attachments are rooted in the acute sense of being a separate creature. "I am alone, so I must put myself first at any cost." *I, me, mine* – these are the ego's watchwords, and when we learn to listen to the mind, we hear them everywhere. The more separate we feel, the more likely we are to get stuck wherever we go.

Fortunately, there is a universal solvent to dissolve all these adhesives. The mind has billions of ways to express its encounter with the dualities of life, but all of them come down to one basic attitude in the mind: "I like this, I don't like that." This response is what keeps the mind moving up and down as it reacts to what is going on around us. To teach the mind to stay even, therefore, we have simply to work on loosening the hold of liking and disliking wherever it comes up during the day. We don't have to analyze; we start simply by not automatically doing what we like and doing cheerfully what we dislike – assuming, of course, that it is beneficial.

If this sounds unpleasant, I agree: it is, at least at first. These are exercises, like sit-ups or weight training: in the category of things we do not for their own sake, but because of the benefits they bring. In the case of loosening likes and dislikes, the benefit is freedom – and it begins to be felt almost immediately. Every time you resist a habitual preference, even in something so apparently minor as eating your broccoli, you are weakening the conditioning of the mind to be happy only with what it likes. Quickly you find yourself no longer compelled to do what you enjoy, but instead enjoying whatever you do.

To avoid misunderstanding, I should make it clear that the Gita isn't recommending anything like asceticism. The Gita counsels a middle path in everything:

> Arjuna, those who eat too much or eat too little, who sleep too much or sleep too little, will not succeed in meditation. But those who are temperate in eating and sleeping, work and recreation, will come to the end of sorrow through meditation. (6:16–17)

In practice, this means we can make solid progress simply by systematically doing what is beneficial, even if we dislike it, and refraining from doing anything that is not beneficial even if we like it. What makes this yoga is its purpose: we are doing these things to make the mind even, by freeing ourselves from the tyranny of likes and dislikes. This is challenging enough without hair shirts and self-mortification, and it is so effective that even those who are not meditating can bring a great deal of freedom into their lives by reducing likes and dislikes.

In fact, you can make a game of this. Juggle with your likes and dislikes: toss them into the air, switch them from hand to hand, keep them moving, don't hold on. You can depend on life to come up with situations that catch you off guard, but if you've learned to juggle with your likes and dislikes, you can always choose how to respond – with people, situations, jobs, everything.

For example, when you go to a restaurant, play with your likes and dislikes and let your partner order for you. When you shop at a supermarket, pick up something nutritious that you dislike. It's a game; your mind doesn't have to take it seriously. When you can play all these games in detachment, you are free. That's artistry.

As you learn to watch your mind during this kind of play, you'll be surprised to see likes and dislikes coming up everywhere. It gives an idea of the tricks your mind has been playing on you. For example, just take one little question: how many times have you returned your Christmas gifts? When I first came to this country, I assumed that stores would be empty after Christmas was over, so the day after Christmas I went with Christine to buy some things we needed. The crowds were bigger than ever, and probably even ruder; they all wanted to return gifts they didn't like. It's a small thing, but even here we can learn to be satisfied with what life sends us, particularly if it comes from someone dear.

The same considerations hold everywhere: the food we eat, the books and papers we read, the magazines we look at, the movies we attend, the TV shows we watch, the conversation we indulge in, the company we keep. There is a choice in all these things. We don't have to be dictated to by rigid likes and dislikes, particularly when they push us in undesirable directions.

Yoga means reducing likes and dislikes like this every day. As a carpenter planes a rough piece of wood, you can smooth out your likes and dislikes whenever you get an opportunity, particularly where other people are concerned. If you do this systematically, it may not take much time to get over most of your likes and dislikes, healing the split in consciousness at deeper and deeper levels.

It's a sobering thought, but not doing this actually widens that split. Most of the time, what we use the mind for is simply to dwell upon ourselves – our needs, our wants, our likes and dislikes – and if that tendency is not resisted, it can quietly get worse. When we yield to a craving or act on an urge, when we act or even talk unkindly, we are sharpening our likes and dislikes, increasing the sense of separateness, and moving farther away from our real Self.

In the case of people who indulge in this kind of thinking often, self-will becomes so inflated that they cannot stand any opposition or contradiction. They find themselves unable to go against their dislikes; they must always have what they like. In such cases the split is becoming wider, which means there are often conflicts even over trifling things. This can reach such an extreme that the person is not able to function in life; living and working with others has become impossible. Sadly, there is really no limit to this because it takes place in consciousness, which has no boundaries. There is a limit to how much potato salad one can eat, but there is no limit to how much we can indulge in thinking about ourselves.

Wherever there is disharmony or personal difficulties, you may be certain that likes and dislikes are involved. When we dislike someone's behavior, for example, what we are really saying is that we would like to regulate that person's mind – make him think the way we do because our way is superior. Particularly in quarrels between two people who are emotionally entangled, this is often the crux of the matter: each wants to control the other's thinking. The Gita says reasonably, You can't regulate the way other people think; it's not possible. Why not try to regulate your own thinking instead?

Here, I think, the Gita makes an important contribution to understanding stress. In this view, the stress we take on ourselves is often due to no more than selfish attachment. At work, for example – assuming that we are talking about psychological rather than physiological stress – what makes a job stressful is often not so much the task itself, but the mind:

dwelling on how much we dislike it, dwelling upon ourselves, worrying, wishing things or people would be different, letting ourselves be thrown between conflicts like a Frisbee. "What has he done to me? What has she done for me?" – always making ourselves the frame of reference. As long as consciousness is divided between *I like this* and *I don't like that, I like him* and *I don't like her,* that division will be a prolific ground for breeding stress. Just as malarial mosquitos flourish in marshy places, stress flourishes in a divided mind.

In this view, nobody makes us insecure except ourselves. Nobody is pouring turmoil into our mind except ourselves, by giving inner significance to events in the light of our own mental makeup. You may remember the observation of an eminent physiologist that I quoted in chapter 2: nobody knows what the external world really is; all that we know is what we experience, our own nervous system. And the nervous system is dumb. It doesn't know how to make choices. Give it pain, it will get roused; give it pleasure, it will get roused, and all the time we think we're reacting to something outside.

When we say "I don't like that person," what we are really saying is, "This is what my nervous system is recording, and I don't like it. If I go near that person, I break out in a rash. If I work with that person, I get migraine. If I live with that person, I cannot sleep." We are not really saying anything about that person; we are talking about the state of our nervous system, saying we don't like to work with our nervous system.

That's the ridiculous side of it. Why should that bother us? As the Gita says over and over, these are reactions between two external objects; why should we jump in?

> When the senses come in contact with sense objects,
>
> a person experiences heat or cold, pleasure or pain.
> These experiences are fleeting; they come and go. Bear
> them patiently, Arjuna. (2:14)

If the cause of personal stress is not outside us but arises from our perception, it follows that by reducing likes and dislikes, we can gradually change the internal significance we attach to external events. Once we do this, we see that events are just events, neither pro nor con, neither for us nor against us. Similarly, people are just people, neither for us nor against us. That is why the Gita says that when we see life as it is, we see that there is no cause for personal sorrow. That one insight brings compassion and the precious capacity to help without judging or getting burned out.

Learning to keep an even mind like this is practicing yoga on the surface of life, in our everyday behavior. But as we go on practicing, behavior is increasingly guided by the higher mind rather than the lower, which means that consciousness is changing. We are healing the split in personality, and gradually the process works deeper, so that what begins as training attention becomes, in time, training of the will, and eventually training of desire. In other words – remembering those

Russian dolls again – the unification of consciousness gradually moves, level by level, deeper and deeper into personality.

There is an intimate connection, therefore, between problems in meditation and problems in daily living. Difficulties in meditation can throw light on everyday problems, and by learning to solve those problems in meditation, we can learn to solve them during the day as well. If you are systematically keeping your mind on an even keel, keeping attention one-pointed on the task at hand, using every opportunity to teach the senses to listen to you, and trying to turn your sensitiveness away from yourself to respond to the needs of others, meditation will deepen rapidly. Soon you will be able to look back and see how many personal problems that pertain to a particular level of consciousness are left behind when you go deeper. Instead of trying to tinker with one problem after another, for which there is no end, we simply move to a deeper level where these problems cannot reach, cannot even follow.

It sounds so simple; it sounds so easy. It is neither simple nor easy, and the challenges increase the deeper we go. Ultimately we hit a wall – a shadowy frontier between what might be called the personal unconscious and the universal or collective unconscious. Beyond that frontier lie our deepest resources, guarded by all the subhuman traits of our evolutionary past. Learning to cross that frontier and move about freely at these depths marks the beginning of the last phase in the unification of consciousness.

◈ *Healing the Unconscious*

I HAVE DESCRIBED the split in consciousness as a wound, a slice through personality from the surface to the core. We have been talking about healing this split near the surface, at the level of behavior, but of course this is a dangerous way to try to heal a wound: patching up the skin alone leaves the inside of the cut to fester. In meditation, however, as the mind becomes one-pointed, the healing work starts from the bottom upward too. We are working in both directions, practicing yoga during the day while filling in the gap deep in consciousness in meditation; when those great projects meet, consciousness is whole and the state of yoga has been attained.

I found a striking illustration of digging through levels of consciousness when reading about one of the deep observation projects launched by the National Science Foundation. Earth scientists from several universities were planning to dig thirty-three thousand feet – about six and a half miles – below the dense gravel of the southern Appalachian mountains, to make a kind of geological window through which to study the tremendous forces that have shaped the region. They were hoping to get practical answers to three big questions: How do resources like petroleum get trapped where they do? How does what they call the underground plumbing system work in distributing vital minerals? And, most urgent, how do major earthquakes occur, and are there safeguards that can be undertaken before an earthquake strikes?

All this reminded me of what can be done in the depths of meditation. There too we can set up a window in consciousness through which we can observe the forces that clash and cooperate, separate and unite, in the unconscious mind. In meditation we are drilling through tremendous strata of resistance, built up layer upon layer over millions of years of evolution – a frustrating endeavor that requires almost infinite patience.

Once we penetrate the collective unconscious, however, we can begin setting up an observation post where we can see why we quarrel, why we get angry, how we get afraid, how negative emotions can be transformed into positive ones, how emotional problems are caused and what is the best way to overcome them, how factors that make us sick can sometimes be reversed to make us whole – in short, to trace the development of action back through thought and feeling to ahamkara, self-will, at the center of personality.

Even the questions of those earth scientists have parallels here. Every human being, for example, has extraordinary resources hidden within; where are they trapped, and why are we not able to get at them and use them? Sometimes these resources have been distributed to areas where the power in them is unavailable; we can learn how they can be released. And we can learn to see the forces that come together to make a human being explode in an earthquake of anger, fear, or hatred. Personality is molded by these deep forces, which surge in everybody's consciousness far below the surface level.

Of course, it takes years of meditation to reach these depths. We begin at the surface of consciousness, and the first shock comes when we break through the surface and find ourselves in an utterly different realm. Like divers in deep waters who lose their sense of up and down, we leave behind the finite phenomena of the sense world on the long descent towards the seabed of consciousness and find ourselves in a vast intervening region that is essentially uncharted. These are murky waters where light doesn't penetrate; for a while our eyes don't function and we cannot make anything out. We have not yet learned to become conscious in the unconscious, and the first thing that is likely to happen is that we let concentration go and fall asleep.

This state can be a kind of Alice's Wonderland. A number of confusing phenomena may take place if concentration wavers. Many people get fascinated by lights, thinking they are beckoning from the other shore. They are very much on this shore. Others hear sounds, often words in no known language, but occasionally meaningful phrases that can prompt a certain kind of person to action. If you wander into these areas in meditation, you are no longer meditating; you are ceding sovereignty to your unconscious mind. In time, you may begin to lose discrimination in daily life as well, doing things that shouldn't be done and failing to do things that should – the classic description of confusion given by St. Paul.

Last Christmas I was watching the crowds at a shopping mall that proclaimed for the season, "The Fantasy Is Real!" It was a perfect illustration of moha: people wandering in a daze, gawking left and right, going nowhere, just looking for something, anything, to capture their attention. Like Macy's, the interior world too is a fairyland of beguiling sights and sensations; the more you look around, the longer you want to stay on, and the longer you stay, the more you want to see. For these and similar reasons, every experienced meditation teacher will remind students repeatedly not to let attention wander, whether in meditation or during the day.

One thing we discover below the surface of consciousness is that the senses are open channels into the mind. Impressions from the external world are flowing constantly into our consciousness. In Sanskrit, any consumption by the senses is called eating, and the mind is considered the sixth sense. In this terminology, even if on the physical level we have only three meals a day, on the thought level the mental body is snacking around the clock, often with an emphasis on junk foods: anger in six flavors, fear soft-boiled and hard, frustration in sizes from small to king-sized. There is even a special menu for dieters: a little resentment, a little malice, a little hostility; everything in small portions, but it all adds up.

We are snacking like this constantly, the Gita would say, and often it amounts to no more than likes and dislikes: "I don't like him, I don't like her, I don't like this, I don't like that." When we indulge in this kind of thinking too often, it helps to remember that, like the body, the mind is what it eats.

Other unpleasant workings of the mind show up too, such as unpleasant memories: what took place in Santa Barbara ten years ago between you and your friend, what he said to you, what you said to her . . . After all, this is the unconscious, the place for things we don't want to be aware of. We mustn't be daunted at what is revealed when we bring light into these dark realms. Things that seem solid and threatening are only shadows, which Sri Krishna promises will be dispelled by the light of wisdom:

> Out of compassion I destroy the darkness of their igno-
> rance. From within them I light the lamp of wisdom
> and dispel all darkness from their lives. (10:11)

As in dreams, the unconscious mind shuffles the cards of our memories and deals us what comes up: there is no system;

there is no order. I had a friend in college who was a poor student but brilliant at cards. I asked him to show me one trick and then tell me how he did it. He shuffled the cards and said, "Take one and don't show it to me."

I did, and he said, "Ace of spades."

"How did you know?" I asked, suitably amazed.

"Look," he said, "I just pushed it towards you. You didn't notice, but you took what I wanted you to." That is what the unconscious does: invite us to take any card and then push what it chooses, usually unpleasant.

When we learn to be conscious in these realms, however, a great challenge comes: we *can* choose. When the unconscious pushes a card at us, expecting us to act on it, we can say, "No, I don't want that one. I know what it is: the king of ill will. I want the queen of good will." In other words, at these depths we begin to have a choice in what to act on and what to turn away from – a choice in what to make more real and what less.

In fact, when the door opens into the unconscious, the world within becomes as real as the world without. The external world is far, far away now, not only in space but in time. It's not a small distance that you have traveled; you have reached a great depth, at which the world within seems much more valid than what you saw on the surface, where everybody thinks everybody else is separate and thinks it natural, "only human," to fight. Now you see that this is not natural, not human; what is natural is to see everybody as one. It's not that the world without becomes less real, but the barrier between without and within falls. It's actually an arbitrary barrier; there is really no division between the outside world and the world within the mind.

Only after breaking through many layers of ignorance do we begin to see how vast this world is. The sea that surges within this small body seems almost limitless. For this experience not to be overwhelming, it is critical to understand what is waiting for us as we sink deeper and deeper into the sea within.

During the monsoon rains in Kerala, when pools and wells overflow and every road is flooded, the more daring boys in my village liked to leap into the deepest, darkest pool they could find from the tallest tree nearby. I was not noted for this kind of daring, partly because I wasn't particularly courageous and partly because I didn't find much appeal in doing something just because it was dangerous. But on one occasion some of my cousins persuaded me to jump from what seemed to me a great height, which they probably considered baby level. Not knowing how to go about it safely, I just stood straight and dropped in as if I were standing at attention. I went in like an arrow. "Easy," I thought. "Simple. All you do is stand at attention and go in."

Then I started coming up. That was a very different story. I strained for the surface for all I was worth, but the more distance I covered, the farther it seemed I had to go. I got panicky, and my lungs began to scream, "We can't take any more!" My head was about to burst and my heart ready to give out – and the daylight at the surface continued to beckon, always just a few strokes away yet out of reach. I decided later that only divine grace could have enabled me to reach the surface alive.

That is how it feels at first to be deep in the unconscious: immeasurable pressure on your mind and the world you know utterly beyond your reach. Yet there is no reason to panic. With practice, descent into these realms becomes straightforward. We glide as gracefully as a diver into a mode of knowing we never suspected, where language begins to break down.

Yet the pressures remain, mostly imposed by desires for personal pleasure, power, and profit – all the desires with which we define ourselves as separate from the rest of life. Most of us live under the honest impression that these desires are freely chosen through rational thinking. Only when we reach a deeper level can we see how many of our private drives are compulsive; we have no say in them at all. Some craving we don't even suspect we have comes up from nowhere and whispers, "You sent for us," and the ego gives its support; the intellect says, "Yes, this is my decision," and the mind agrees, "Right, this is what I want." And then the body carries it out. All the levels of personality get in on the act – each dancing to the tune of a compulsion that has no real life of its own, that is nothing more than a deeply conditioned habit.

All this is just the opposite of the way these levels are intended to interact:

> The senses are higher than the body, and the mind
> higher than the senses; above the mind is the intellect
> [buddhi], and above the intellect is the Atman. Thus,
> knowing that which is supreme, let the Atman rule the
> ego, and slay the fierce enemy that is selfish desire.
> (3:42–43)

Seeing this brings immense motivation. After all, nobody likes to be manipulated like this, made to believe that you are acting on your own, living on your own, thinking on your own, when you actually have nothing to do with it.

Like the deep ocean, this is a silent world so far as the senses are concerned. To the inner ear, however, it is another story. All too soon you become aware of the hubbub these desires raise in the mind. If private urges could be expressed in terms of noise, a craving for fries might rate fifty decibels, the level of ordinary conversation; for a pint of Guinness, maybe sixty. The urge for a hot fudge sundae might rate seventy-five decibels, and a raucous, insistent desire like sex would be as deafening as a rock concert. We have innumerable urges like this, which makes the mind as noisy as a busy airport: urges arriving, urges taking off, long flights, short flights, such chaos and discord that it's almost impossible to find someplace quiet. When anybody asks why we don't hear the still, small voices of conscience and common sense, this is the answer: the cacophony of the physical urges and agitation that goes on in the mind.

This is why, to go deeper, the mind has to quiet down. In fact, below a certain depth in meditation it really has no choice. If we can sustain unbroken concentration at this depth, the mind gives up and grows still. "You go ahead, boss," it says; "I'll just sit here and rest. I'm tired with all this concentration." You can actually watch the mind spreading newspapers on a park bench and then lying down. You go on ahead, and when you look back you can see, sure enough, the mind is fast asleep. But this does not mean there is no awareness: in this state you are acutely aware of being more alert and wakeful than on the surface, with the mind chattering away. "Mind" here refers simply to an inner instrument of consciousness, just as the body is the external instrument. In deep concentration that instrument is temporarily unplugged, allowing the transcendental faculty of knowing to slowly wake up.

Then comes a thrilling development: you begin to sense a whisper saying that you are not a finite creature, not a separate fragment of life but part of the whole. You cannot locate the source of that whisper, but you slowly become aware that there is a presence within whom you have ignored, of whose existence you have not even known, who is trying to talk to you. Years ago, when I first tried talking to my nieces in India with a landline phone – a distance of almost nine thousand miles – I could barely hear; I finally had to ask the operator to get us another connection. Even then I couldn't recognize their voices; I had to guess: "Is this little Geetha?" She replied, "I'm no longer little, Uncle." Only then did I recognize her. It is like that in the unconscious, too. Finally you are able to recognize that it is your real voice speaking to you; this ego has been a ventriloquist. It is then that you realize you are drawing closer to your real Self.

For a long time, however, you may feel you are on what used to be called a party line. This kind of telephone service was still common in the U.S. – at least in Kansas – when I arrived in 1959: the phone company often provided only one line to a number of houses, which meant that everyone had to share. When the phone rang, anyone on the block could answer – and then, if they chose, they could quietly stay on the line to catch the latest news. In a small town, the local school for scandal seemed able to keep tabs on everyone.

The universal unconscious can feel like that too, flooded with discordant voices and disagreeable tones. Through merciful providence, we cannot eavesdrop on the conversations in the unconscious until we have developed a good measure of detachment and compassion, for it can be distressing to see the darker side of personality right there within us. It is for our own well-being that a dense curtain hides the unconscious until we are ready to take this dark side on.

For it is here, near the source of the split in personality, that we begin to see that the real causes of our inner conflicts have very little to do with parents or partner or friends or colleagues or anything else outside. These conflicts have unlisted numbers, so we haven't been able to trace the calls. It can fill you with regret, flood you with guilt, to discover the subterranean urges that are the real culprits.

But there is no need to take this personally. These urges are universal, inherited as part of our biological legacy. Only the details are personal, to the extent we have acted on them in our lives. That is why even to reach this stage we need enough detachment to look upon our own failings with the same compassion we give others – remembering always that our real Self, everyone's real Self, is ever pure, completely untouched by even the most serious lapse:

> This supreme Self is without a beginning, undifferentiated, deathless. Though it dwells in the body, Arjuna, it neither acts nor is touched by action. As space pervades the cosmos but remains unstained, the Self can never be tainted though it dwells in every creature.
> (13:31–32)

I read somewhere that when the devil appeared before Martin Luther, he threw his ink stand at him. The idea behind this is that the devil is not you, but somebody outside whom you can fight. The Gita expresses this positively by referring to the idea of levels of reality. To the extent we identify ourselves with the selfish side of personality, that side of us is real; but once we identify ourselves with the selfless part, the negative side no longer exists.

Other interesting phenomena take place at this depth in consciousness. For one, you begin to observe some of the signals between levels of personality that formerly went unseen. It's a fascinating observation. Since you are detached now, no longer personally involved, you can intercept these signals and decode them. An impulse is received from the outside world that is painful or upsetting – say, somebody has criticized you severely – and the transmitting station sends the message: "Help! Distress!"

But the message passes through half a dozen stations, and you can listen in and even add your own two cents along the way. At the first station, you can moderate the message a little: "Do you have to be so angry?" Next station: "Why not try to show a little more self-control?" By the third station the signal is fifty percent anger, fifty percent compassion, and when it finally reaches the destination, it reads, "Forgive. Forbear." You are freeing the nervous system from the tyranny of likes and dislikes.

When you are at home in the unconscious, you can actually observe when a new track like this is being laid. The nervous system is being reconditioned; traffic is being rerouted, and the previous pathways fall into disuse like abandoned roads.

When Christine and I lived in Berkeley we used to take long walks in the hills above the Lawrence Radiation Lab, and one day we came across an old road and decided to see where it led. To our surprise, a military chap appeared from nowhere and asked sternly, "Where do you think you are going?"

We explained innocently that I taught at the university and we were just following the road. He said, "That's not a road any more. This is private property" – which it wasn't, really; it belonged to my university, and we were allowing it to be used by the Department of Defense. I started to explain that but decided not to press the point, and we were ushered out as possible spies.

By now, I imagine, that road is so overgrown that no one will mistake it for a road again. That is what happens to compulsions when you lay a new track: if you keep rerouting the traffic, the old tracks gradually fade into grassy meadow again. (On the other hand, when you've put in a lot of hard work laying a new track and then get angry or upset or uncooperative, what you are doing is tearing up what you have built – another illustration of the intimate connection between meditation and the disciplines of yoga during the day.)

All these tracks are finely connected, making the mind a tangled network. Even what seem to be irrelevant distractions are connected with deeper elements of personality that in Sanskrit are called *samskaras*: mental formations that have been built up over years and years of conditioning by thinking and acting in a particular way. Much as the repeating patterns of waves in the ocean are shaped by sandbars deep below, many superficial habits and mannerisms are shaped by the deep patterns of samskaras, which in turn are shaped and connected with ones that are deeper still.

It is amazing to observe these connections, because judging by behavior, nobody would suspect a relationship. Samskaras are like chameleons; they take the color of their context. When you think you have caught one and look closely to try to make it out, it blends into the background and then sits there looking at you smugly and chewing gum, as if to say, "Who, me?" That's why I say there is no study on earth more fascinating than the mind. It's such a complex system that it is easy to get lost in it and to get on the wrong track.

Samskaras often nourish each other. Resentment, self-will, and insecurity, for example, feed on each other, developing a whole family of negative habits. Whenever you see a pronounced samskara, you can be reasonably sure it has brought certain ancillary samskaras along with it. Meditation becomes like a glass-bottom boat, where you can sit in safety and watch thoughts rise to the surface like bubbles from deep below. The bubbles are distractions, coming from a huge shark of a samskara swimming underneath. There is probably no end to the number of bubbles on the surface, but by and large, the Gita focuses on three major sources: not always the same three, but always including the Top Two: lust and anger. The

Gita doesn't call these sharks, of course. It uses even stronger language:

> There are three gates to this self-destructive hell: lust,
> anger, and greed. Renounce these three! Those who
> escape from these three gates of darkness, Arjuna, seek
> what is highest and attain life's goal. (16:21–22)

Sometimes the third of these samskaras is fear, sometimes greed, but in every case the parent samskara – the godfather, if you like – is self-will, the illusion of separateness. Another of its child samskaras is insecurity, which most people find trivial. It is not; it reaches deep into consciousness. Even such apparently opposite traits as belligerence and arrogance are simply attempts to compensate for this deep sense of feeling isolated and incomplete. When you are working with others and you feel you know better, you get arrogant, which undermines whatever you might have to contribute; where you feel you don't have anything to contribute, you become apologetic, afraid to oppose anyone or to offer helpful criticism. Either way, insecurity brings difficulties into almost every relationship.

In this way, a whole network of samskaras arises from a single source. Whenever you let insecurity in, it brings along its whole staff: jealousy, competition, and their assistants, relatives, and friends, each of which can start a network of its own. Jealousy, for example – I think Shakespeare was right in calling it a monster. It can completely wreck your peace of mind. You're always comparing yourself with others; wherever you are, you are not at home with yourself; you are wishing you were someone else. It not only ruins relationships; it can even bring in physical problems. There are diseases that physicians call "great imitators" because they mimic other ailments. Insecurity is a great imitator: it can simulate a number of physical problems, and when physical problems are simulated for a long time, they become real.

When you come face to face with a samskara, it has tremendous power. It's no longer able to conceal itself, so all its power is exposed. Until we reach this depth, a samskara like sex can hide behind masks and express itself in euphemistic language: "I just like to be close to her"; "I just like working with him." But once you get face to face with the samskara, it drops all attempts to dissemble and just says, "S-e-x" – and repeats it, in case you didn't hear.

This touches a subtle point. As long as a samskara can masquerade, you can't see an opponent to fight. You are there in the boxing ring, you have your boxing trunks and whatever it is they stuff into your mouth, the referee and crowds are waiting, but there is no opponent in sight. Yet still you are getting hit. The samskara lands a blow and you want to hit back, but there is nobody to swing at. I would say it is much better to have an opponent you can see, however grisly he may look. It's much better to see your weaknesses clearly than to let them knock you about while you turn a blind eye and consider your-self free.

I should make it clear here that there is nothing wrong with sex or any other powerful desire so long as we are in control and don't allow it to become destructive. Ultimately, these urges are just raw energy like electricity, neither good nor bad. But electricity can light a house or electrocute the tenant, so we should be the ones who say how that energy is used. In everything, the goal of yoga is freedom, the complete trans-formation of every conditioned impulse and response.

When a compulsion comes to the surface at this stage, therefore, that is a positive development. You have been heal-ing the split in the depths of consciousness; now no more than a shallow cut remains at the surface. This raises a techni-cal problem: how to unite the rest. This cannot be done through meditation alone; meditation can only go so far. Then how do we complete the healing?

The answer is, through deliberate behavior during the day. We act as if we were completely dedicated to the spiritual life, even if we have reservations. We act as if we had no selfish mo-tives; we behave as if we had no conflicts. We give our best at work, we give unwavering love and support to partner and family and friends, and of course we are absolutely systematic about meditation and our other spiritual disciplines. In all such ways, the deep changes we have made in consciousness are being translated into a new pattern of external behavior.

You may remember an idea we explored earlier, that experience has two faces, one objective and one interior. The Sanskrit term, which we encountered earlier, is *namarupa,* literally "name and form." The practical application here is that even if we could meditate twenty-four hours a day, that would not enable us to transform consciousness, because the form in consciousness and its external expression are conjoined twins. It's not enough to transform rupa; we must also transform nama. That's why yoga requires both internal and external disciplines to unify consciousness and quieten the mind.

Brooding on oneself, for example, is a conditioned response to many kinds of events. There are other ways to respond, but this can become a predisposition – a samskara. When the track of a new response has been laid deep in the mind, there is still some momentum from past behavior, the way a potter's wheel continues to spin awhile after the potter has walked away. If you feel a little depressed one day, the old pattern is still there: you just want to go to your room, shut the door, and sleep your head off.

To complete the healing, what you do at that time is just the opposite of what the samskara demands. You go and work, preferably at something selfless with other people; if you want to walk slowly and brood over your problems, you go out for a long, fast walk or even for a run. If you are with people, you don't withdraw; you listen carefully to whatever they have to say, even if you find it boring, and come up with a considerate response. Your attention will try to wander again and again: this is *not* what the mind wants to do. You just tell your mind, "Sorry, you're not me – and this is what we're going to do, so you may as well enjoy it." The change has been made in consciousness, at the level of the will; there is just a bit more work to be done on the physical level.

I don't mean to be misleading with such illustrations. To reach this point is far from easy; in India, one is considered blessed to get this far in a lifetime. After all, the essence of a compulsion is that we have no say in it, and here we are talking about transforming all compulsions deep in the unconscious, where by definition we are *not* conscious, cannot see, have no volition to bring to bear. That it can be done at all is a miracle.

The Gita throws light on the magnitude of this challenge in haunting words. Arjuna asks, "What makes us act on these compulsions, Krishna? What power compels us, even against our will?" And Sri Krishna replies:

It is selfish desire and anger, arising from the guna of rajas; these are the appetites and evils which threaten a person in this life.

Just as a fire is covered by smoke and a mirror obscured by dust, just as the embryo rests deep within the womb, knowledge is hidden by selfish desire – hidden, Arjuna, by this unquenchable fire for self-satisfaction, the inveterate enemy of the wise.

Selfish desire is found in the senses, mind, and intellect, misleading them and burying the understanding in delusion. Fight with all your strength, Arjuna! Controlling your senses, conquer your enemy, the destroyer of knowledge and realization. (3:37–41)

No outside force is compelling us, Sri Krishna says; we are driven by our own desires. *Kama* is usually translated as lust, which is accurate enough, but just as we speak of the lust for money or pleasure or power, the real meaning of *kama* is broader and more pervasive than sexual desire. It refers to the blind drive to satisfy self-will, to have our way, to get what we want regardless of the cost. The mind is saturated with desires prompted by this drive, with advertising and the mass media constantly adding fuel to the fire; and every day, in the depths of our consciousness, we are reminded that these fires are unquenchable: it simply is not possible to satisfy all the fantasies that run through the mind, which promise to bring happiness from something outside and can only make us desperate for more. That is why the Gita keeps insisting on the intimate link between selfish desire and anger, which builds up the more we want and the less we get.

Selfish desire hides in all levels of personality, Sri Krishna says – senses, mind, intellect, and ego or self-will – and at each level, as smoke hides fire, lust and anger hide the wisdom that is our native state.

Years ago a terrible fire broke out in the Oakland hills, and the tragic spectacle of smoke covering the East Bay brought these verses vividly to mind. It was a terrible sight. Behind the stately old Claremont Hotel, where Christine and I used to walk, a huge whirlpool of smoke smoldered up to the clouds. Several people were killed and nearly four thousand families left homeless, their houses reduced to ashes, and the Bay Area was covered by a pall of soot.

This is also what happens in the world within, the Gita says: the dense pall of selfish desire hides the wisdom that shines in the depths of human consciousness. When these destructive passions are given license in the mind, they destroy our home; we become outcasts in our own consciousness, unable to find security anywhere. And as dust hides our face in a mirror, we can't see ourselves as we are; we see only the body, not the Self within.

Therefore, Sri Krishna says, selfish desire and anger are our perpetual enemies. In the millions of forms that these dark drives take to beguile and confuse us, they will work themselves deeper and deeper into consciousness until we drive them out once and for all. The more we try to get them out of our system by indulging them, the deeper they will worm their way in. That is why we have no choice but to destroy these enemies, which are eating away incessantly at the love and wisdom hidden within.

◈ *Life After Life*

ARJUNA IS A warrior, but at this point even he must have doubts about being equal to this challenge. He asks earnestly,

> Krishna, what happens to one who has faith but who lacks self-control and wanders from the path, not attaining success in yoga? If one becomes deluded on the spiritual path, will he lose both worlds, like a cloud scattered in the sky? Krishna, you can dispel all doubts; remove this doubt that binds me. (6:37–39)

This is a heartbreaking question. Arjuna is asking, "If I stake everything on this impossible goal and fail to achieve it, will I lose everything I have gambled? Will I be banished from the pleasures of this world and from spiritual fulfillment too?" It's a brilliant question, and Sri Krishna answers with infinite compassion:

Arjuna, my son, such a person will not be destroyed. No one who does good work will ever come to a bad end, either here or in the world to come. When such people die, they are reborn into a home that is pure and prosperous. Or they may be born into a family where meditation is practiced; to be born into such a family is extremely rare. The wisdom they have acquired in previous lives will be reawakened, Arjuna, and they will strive even harder for Self-realization. Indeed, they will be driven on by the strength of their past disciplines. (6:40–44)

To appreciate this answer, we need a deeper understanding of the Gita's view of life and death.

In Indian thought, the death of the body is not the end of life; it is only the end of one chapter in a long, long story. Just as we say a day has twenty-four hours, meaning by "day" the period of nighttime as well as that of daylight, similarly the Gita would say that life in the fullest sense includes both life and death. In a poetic outburst, the Upanishads say we come into embodied existence and leave it again and again like a fish swimming back and forth from one bank of a river to the other. The Gita is less poetic but perhaps more clear:

Death is inevitable for the living; birth is inevitable for the dead. Since these are unavoidable, you should not sorrow. Every creature is unmanifested at first and then attains manifestation. When its end has come, it again

becomes unmanifested. What is there to lament in this?
(2:27–28)

In this view, each of us has died many millions of times, and the fear of that experience lurks in the utmost depths of our consciousness. Death is not an undiscovered country; we have been there and back more often than we can remember, but always without understanding, blinded by our identification with the body. If we understood its promise, death would hold no fear. It is good to face death with courage, but that is not enough; we must learn to face it with understanding. We must learn to see through death. That is the ultimate message of the Gita: that when death comes, as it must, we can make it a door to a better future.

Even from a biological perspective, the death of the body is not an event that takes place on a particular day at a particular moment. Death is a continuous process. While I am writing this, while you are reading it, each of us is quietly undergoing the process of dying that is inherent in all physical creatures.

In one of his poems, Keats uses a special figure of speech that assumes the future has already happened: "The two brothers and their murdered man rode past fair Florence." This may be an unusual device in literature, but it could be applied to all of us. The moment we were born, the process of dying began its race with life. For a while this process cannot keep pace with physical growth, but by the time we are in our teens or twenties the body begins a slow deterioration, barely visible at first but ever present. Eventually, however much we may resist, this body will be unable to perform its natural functions. Then, like an old jacket that is falling apart, it will need to be cast aside:

> As one abandons worn-out clothes and acquires new
> ones, so when the body is worn out a new one is
> acquired by the Self, who lives within. (2:22)

There is no need to be bewildered or distressed by this, Sri Krishna urges. It is natural and inevitable that the body die some day; the body is physical and obeys physical laws. But we do not die; we are simply removing a jacket.

Knowing death walks by our side does not subtract from life. It is when we forget this that we do foolish things, harmful things, waste our time. When we remember, every day becomes important; every minute is precious. Teresa of Avila, a very practical woman, kept a skull on her desk to remind her that she could not afford to lose a single day. It is not a grisly symbol; it's a rich reminder of the value of life and the reckless profligacy with which we waste our days.

But what dies and what survives? We know the Atman is beyond birth and death, beyond change altogether. The part of personality that continues is carried in the subtle body, the levels of consciousness that remain when the physical body is shed – a bundle of wisdom and ignorance, faith and experience, fears and hopes and desires, all held together by the ego's claim that this is who we are.

Since the subtle body is energy, it doesn't die. We know that matter and energy are interchangeable; all that happens at death is that the material body breaks down into its chemical components and the mental energy bound to it is released back into cosmic energy. For the illumined man or woman this can be a matter of choice – something that can be managed consciously – and at one point Sri Krishna even gives Arjuna a crash course in how to die:

> Remembering me at the time of death, close down the
> doors of the senses and place the mind in the heart.
> Then, while absorbed in meditation, focus all energy
> upwards to the head. Repeating in this state the divine
> name, the syllable *Om* that represents the changeless
> Brahman, you will go forth from the body and attain
> the supreme goal. (8:12–13)

Here, vitality is being withdrawn consciously, level by level, into the very core of personality. This is easy to visualize with those Russian dolls. First, consciousness is withdrawn from the body and senses into the mind: the outermost doll is unscrewed and removed. At this point, though the sense organs and nervous system may be intact, the sense world no longer registers; awareness is confined to the mind, the world within, as in the dreaming state.

Then consciousness is withdrawn deeper, from the senses into the mind, then from the mind into buddhi, the higher mind, and finally into what is called the causal body, the seat of I-consciousness. It's like taking off an overcoat button by button, then removing your jacket, and finally your pullover, folding each piece carefully and setting it aside.

As you can see, this is much the same process as when attention is withdrawn in profound meditation. Of course, in meditation a little vitality remains in the body to keep it alive. But this is not a necessary connection, and when you learn to withdraw consciousness like this intentionally, you become acutely aware that you are still alive in this state – much more alive, in fact, than when identified with the body.

The language in these verses is suggestive. Krishna doesn't use the word for death; he says "at the time of your final journey." This is not the euphemism it would be in English. Just as one might go to Europe or South America, the dying person has booked passage to some other level of consciousness, as real as a place on the map. For those who have attained Self-realization, that journey leads to a state beyond change, which Sri Krishna calls simply "my home":

> Those who realize life's goal know that I am unmanifested and unchanging. Having come home to me, they are not born separate again. (8:21)

To reach this state, however, requires a mind that doesn't

move in the slightest, either with fear or with personal attachment. All our faculties must be "united by the power of yoga," which requires a lifetime of devoted, dedicated effort. It is the accumulated thrust of the practice of meditation day in and day out that prepares us to unite all our consciousness for this journey, so that when the time comes, our luggage is packed and our papers in order and we are ready to go. Then, Krishna promises, the divine presence within us will draw us like a magnet, and we will be united with our real Self.

Arjuna, however, is asking what happens when we have not achieved this supreme state. Then the same process takes place, but involuntarily. Anyone who has been at the side of a dying person has seen consciousness withdrawn like this until the senses seem to have closed down. Even then, the Gita maintains, that person is still very much alive, and often able to absorb some of what is going on. That is why in many cultures the scriptures are read aloud over a dying person: the words do go in, and provide some guidance for the journey. Inevitably, however, the connection is finally broken – a kind of surgery in which the physical body is separated from the subtle body. When this operation is complete, awareness is confined completely within the subtle body, which is on its own at last.

This is not easy to understand, but when its meaning is absorbed, death loses its terrors. Of course, the body is likely to suffer, but from the spiritual point of view, most of the problems of dying come from the inability to let go. This is not something done consciously; it has to be done in the unconscious. Here the Upanishads have a wonderful simile. Watch a caterpillar as it comes to the end of a leaf: it reaches out and attaches itself to the next leaf before letting the first one go. Similarly, if we understand what is happening at this point, we can reach out to the future that death promises us and not cling to the body that is failing. It's like giving up an old pullover in exchange for a new cashmere: there is no sacrifice; you just let the old one go. All your attention is focused on where you are going; there is no attention on what you are leaving behind, which means there is no clinging. It's not so much that you're not afraid of death; the question simply doesn't arise.

> As one abandons worn-out clothes and acquires new
> ones, so when the body is worn out a new one is
> acquired by the Self, who lives within. (2:22)

When the body dies, for a while the poor ego is not even aware that it is gone. It's a bit like the phenomenon of phantom limb, when someone who has lost an arm or leg feels an itch in a part of the body that is no longer there. The physical body is gone, but its image in the subtle body persists for a while as a kind of aftereffect. Gradually, however, these impressions fade and awareness drifts free of worldly time, much as the mind does in a dream. The person now lives entirely in the subtle body, which, as we saw earlier, carries a meticulously documented library of all our past thoughts, words, and actions – in other words, our samskaras.

We have talked about samskaras, but I haven't emphasized the dynamic side. A samskara is a conditioned response built up over millions of repetitions. Samskaras are like poison oak in the mind: whenever we do or think something that is self-centered, a stain is left that makes the mind itch, driving us into action when circumstances arise that bring those hidden tendencies into play.

Anger makes a good illustration. Whenever we get angry, we make it easier to yield to anger next time. If it is not resisted, that impulse becomes a habit. Eventually it may even become a compulsion, which means we are angry always. Oddly, this predilection to anger seems to attract people eager to provoke it. But those with a pronounced anger samskara don't really need provocation; one word out of place and they will explode.

It is the same with every samskara, major and minor. Each lies dormant in the mind until circumstances arise where it can be expressed, and every time it is expressed, the samskara gets stronger. You can see why samskaras are often likened to seeds. As an acorn contains the genetic potential to grow into a huge oak tree when it gets an environment that can supply the nutrients it needs, each samskara is a seed of potential action ready to sprout and grow when circumstances are right.

While we are alive, every day is full of opportunities for

this. And each time, we have a choice: shall I resist this impulse and weaken it, or shall I act on it and make it stronger? Of course, since samskaras are conditioned, we usually don't see that we have a choice, and so our samskaras get stronger. But the choice is always there – while we are alive.

After death, however, when we are confined to the subtle body, it is another story. In this state the mind is reverberating with samskaras that have no way to express themselves – samskaras bursting with potential to act, like the electrical charge built up in a thundercloud. We can think of a thundercloud as waiting for the right conditions to release an explosion of lightning; in much the same way, the subtle body waits for circumstances that will allow its samskaras to be discharged. If we have accumulated a lot of anger in this life, for example, the conditioning carried by our samskaras needs to be matched to a context where we will have angry parents, an angry partner, angry neighbors, an angry mail carrier, and an angry dog. It's a ruthless analysis: we can't blame anybody else. If we are full of anger, we must have a context next time around in which we can choose not to be angry when provoked. Otherwise, how could we learn?

In other words, after death we are entered in a kind of cosmic matching service in which we choose our next birth – except, of course, that at this time, not having a body, we're not really able to choose. What we get is determined by the consequences of our previous choices: everything that we have done, said, and thought in life before.

In this state we get a chance to look – in fact, are forced to look – at our past choices and learn from them if possible. I can't watch *A Christmas Carol* without thinking of this. Faced with the consequences of his past decisions, Scrooge piteously asks the Ghost of Christmas Yet to Come, "Are these the shadows of the things that will be, or are they shadows of things that may be, only?" He begs for a chance to change – and, of course, he gets one when the next day dawns. Similarly, after death we get a chance to see what mistakes we have committed so that we can resolve not to make them again. If I have a strong anger samskara that I have directed towards my parents, I will be drawn into a context where my children will be angry against me. If I have been a difficult son, I will have a difficult son next time around.

This is often considered a karmic payback: we get what we have earned, reap what we have sown. But karma is essentially an opportunity to learn. We can let situations work against us, strengthening our negative samskaras, or we can turn challenges and adversities into opportunities to undo those samskaras and work ourselves free. This holds true for all our samskaras, which is why, whenever we find ourselves in a difficult situation, we should never try to run away but learn to face it calmly, courageously, and compassionately.

In effect, then, it is this pool of samskaras – the contents of consciousness at the end of life – that decides our destiny in the next. We are going to pick up everything just where we left off. The Gita expresses this with a beautiful image:

> An eternal part of me enters into the world, assuming
> the powers of action and perception and a mind made
> of prakriti. When the divine Self enters and leaves a
> body, it takes these along as the wind carries a scent
> from place to place. (15:7–8)

To give a more down-to-earth illustration, when I once went to pick up a suit at the cleaners, the man gave me a little envelope along with it. Inside were a few coins and a quotation from the Gita. "I found these in your pocket," he explained. "People leave a lot of things in their pockets when they come here."

"What kinds of things?" I asked.

He shrugged. "Oh," he said, "you'd be surprised: money, checks, maybe a watch or some jewelry, sometimes racing tips – top secret, you know, 'eyes only.'"

That's a good comparison for the contents of consciousness. When the subtle body goes to the cleaners, all kinds of things are left in the pockets: a little craving for food, some desire for profit, a weakness for pleasure, a hankering after prestige. The Cosmic Cleaner carefully collects them all and puts them in a packet for us; when we show up to claim the suit, we get the packet too.

Now we are getting back to Arjuna's original question. Sri Krishna is saying, "If, after meditating for some years, you find yourself blocked by your samskaras, I'll chalk up credit for the progress you have made." It's like what American stores call a layaway plan. We didn't have anything like that in India when I came to the U.S., so I was surprised at the enthusiastic response I got when I went to one of these big stores in San Francisco with Christine and looked at something rather expensive. "Would you like to buy this?" the clerk asked. "It's only sixty dollars."

"I haven't even got six," I replied.

"That's all right," she assured me cheerfully. "Can you pay five? That's enough to cover the first payment. We will lay it away for you, and you come and pay five dollars every month. In a year it's yours."

It is the same after death: this is layaway sadhana. If we can't make the full payment for Self-realization in this life, the subtle body will hold all our payments as credit towards the next installment in our next life.

In other words, according to the Gita, any interest in the spiritual life that we feel today is not a sudden development. It has been laid away and we simply haven't claimed it. We go along for twenty or thirty years completely unmindful of our previous investment, playing games at school, traveling about, going surfing, making money, learning all kinds of skills without a thought of meditation. Then one day we go to the bookstore and see the Bhagavad Gita or hear a talk on the *Imitation of Christ* and something clicks. We have received a little reminder by subtle mail: "You have a packet laid away. Please come and pick it up." Some words from the book or talk get in and we go home dazed. We think about them, ponder them, and a little window in consciousness opens; we say to ourselves, "Maybe I should give this meditation a try."

Then, swiftly, the old zest for the spiritual life returns. After a year or two of meditation, we find there has been a tremendous deepening of consciousness. We see life differently; our values have become more selfless and our aspirations more spiritual. This is simply regaining what we had already learned. We haven't added to our wisdom; it was lying there within us and we have just picked it up again. Self-realization is not attained by the efforts of one lifetime; it comes through the sustained effort we have made over many, many lives.

One of the surest signs of this is to be born in a good family, of good parents, who will help us by their personal example to lead the spiritual life. If our layaway contributions have been substantial, Sri Krishna says, there is no greater privilege in life than to be born into a home where one or both parents meditate, because it gives a flying start. Such a situation is extremely rare, but whenever anyone takes to meditation, the parents deserve a little credit too. The debt may not be obvious

– parents can help even by opposing us. Sometimes we seem not to have made the best choice in our parents; often they may seem not to have made the best choice in us. But nobody gets a lemon. We have made the choices by the kind of person we were the last time around, and everybody gets what he or she needs to grow.

In other words, there is much more to this layaway packet than a bundle of samskaras. We also pick up whatever wisdom we have gained:

> The wisdom they have acquired in previous lives will be
> reawakened, Arjuna, and they will strive even harder
> for Self-realization. (6:43)

The Sanskrit is precise: "wisdom" here is buddhi, the so-called higher mind, which retains not merely what we have learned but the very capacity to learn from past mistakes and avoid past pitfalls, developed by the detached intellect in life after life. Detached intelligence is the very source of wisdom, and in our next birth that acquired wisdom awakens to guide us to the extent we listen to it, not so much in the head as in the heart.

Even if we try to ignore this guidance and plunge into all kinds of selfish pursuits, Sri Krishna says, the momentum of what we have learned is so powerful that it can sweep our dalliance aside and take us in the right direction. I have known people like that; the reversal can be quite dramatic.

Not even our dearest, the Buddha says, can come with us after death. Who does come with us? Our karma. It is not a dead thing; it is a living presence. This has nothing to do with supernatural forces. Karma is simply cause and effect. There is nothing we can get away with. Every harmful word, every hostile deed, will walk with us after death; similarly, all the kindness and goodness we have shown, all the selfless service we have done, will walk with us as a friend, supporting us and making the future happier.

This leaves everything in our hands. When you understand the miracle of it, you see there is no outward force on which your life is dependent. We can so regulate our present life that we can continue it right where we leave off: the choice is up to us.

◇ The Long Journey
of Evolution

EVER SINCE HUMAN beings began telling tales around the evening fire, I imagine, life has been compared with a journey – a poignant image that no one has portrayed more vividly than the Persian poet and mathematician Omar Kháyyám, whose *Rubáiyát* has been a favorite of mine since I discovered the English versions of Edward Fitz-Gerald in my teens. It was only much later that a Muslim friend revealed to me the Sufi symbolism so easily misunderstood in a worldly reading. The poet compares life on earth with a caravanserai, a travelers' waystation on the long journey of the soul towards God:

> Think, in this battered Caravanserai
> Whose Portals are alternate Night and Day,
>   How Sultán after Sultán with his Pomp
> Abode his destin'd Hour, and went his way.

One Moment in Annihilation's Waste,

One Moment, of the Well of Life to taste –

    The Stars are setting and the Caravan

Starts for the Dawn of Nothing – Oh, make haste!

The Bird of Time has but a little way

To fly – and Lo! the Bird is on the Wing.

The Gita extends this metaphor to the beginning and end of time. Life is a journey over billions of years: the great chain of being, a kind of spiritual evolution in which consciousness emerges from inanimate matter through eons of biological experimentation. At the human level comes the capacity for fully unconditioned awareness and Self-realization. In this way, from the lowest form of life upwards, each creature may be seen as trying to project itself into a higher level of life.

On this scale the human being is the "roof and crown" of creation, but not in the sense the Victorian poets meant. We have not inherited dominion over nature, the Gita would say, but have evolved to the responsibility of trusteeship for ourselves and the rest of life. We have the capacity, and therefore the evolutionary duty, to take our destiny as individuals into our own hands, and thereby help guide life to its fullest potential. *Homo sapiens* represents a stage in evolution halfway between our biological nature and what we can become. We bear both the imprint of the biological level from which we have risen and the latent capacity to realize the full potential of this remarkable brain and mind with which we have been born – life after life, as we have seen, in a long, long ascent of spiritual growth.

From this point of view, any individual who lives mostly for satisfying the senses has barely risen above the animal level, where behavior is dictated by the senses and instincts. I had a convincing insight into this when my mother and I were living on the Nilgiris or Blue Mountains in India. Since I was away at university much of the year, I got two Alsatian dogs to keep my mother company. My family has been vegetarian for generations, so my mother said reasonably, "You can bring in the dogs, but I'm going to make them vegetarian." Our English neighbors joked about it, but our dogs kept in excellent health, unlike the other Alsatians near us, and they were remarkably self-controlled. They never got into trouble with people on the road as the other dogs did, and they never got into fights. Now and then our walks would take us past a pack of wild dogs, which are ferocious animals, but our Alsatians wouldn't even take notice of them; they would just walk on. An English friend teased me by saying their diet had made them cowards, which made me a little anxious until a dramatic incident convinced me otherwise.

One night during the mating season our male dog disappeared. He had never gone off like that before, so we all went in search of him but couldn't find him. Towards morning he came back bleeding from bruises and wounds all over his body. People from a nearby village told us he had gone after a female in heat that had been surrounded by a pack of these wild dogs and had fought against every one of them to get her. He was mauled so badly that we were certain he would die. But on the following night he disappeared again, back to the same place.

I learned a lesson that day: in an animal, sex is an irresistible compulsion, against which it can do nothing even under threat of pain or death. It brought home the Gita's point that any person who is driven by the senses is becoming an animal again. That is why the Gita says that whatever sensory urge we are driven by, if we cannot control it – not suppress it, but simply have a say in it – we are living at the lowest end of our human potential. Here is the war within again: either master the senses or be mastered by them.

According to the Gita, it is the same with anger: the moment we become angry, we have gone back to the animal level. The point is that as human beings, we have a choice. When somebody gets angry with us and we remain calm instead of retaliating, we have broken this link with the animal for the moment and risen a bit higher on our own personal ladder of evolution. Every human being has this choice in every circumstance, the Gita would say: either to remain at the animal level or to move towards fully human behavior by controlling anger, hatred, and violence.

This is a tall order, of course, but isn't this what great teachers like Jesus and the Compassionate Buddha have taught too? The difference – perhaps an appealing one today – is that the Gita does not present this as simply a moral choice and judge us when we fail in it. These choices are checkpoints on our evolutionary journey, opportunities to move away from what we have been conditioned to be and towards unconditioned freedom.

The Forces of Evolution

The Gita has a far-reaching theory behind this view. In the Gita's cosmology, remember, before the phenomenal world came into existence there was only undifferentiated consciousness – the indivisible, immutable reality that is our native state. As in modern cosmology, the process of creation began when the equilibrium of this state was disturbed, differentiating this primordial energy into three states called gunas: *tamas,* inertia; *rajas,* energy; and *sattva,* law. At the moment of creation these three modes began to interact, producing all kinds of combinations. Everything in the phenomenal world is an expression of these three gunas in different proportions, and evolution progresses from inertia through energy into law. Pure consciousness is still and undifferentiated, though full of limitless potential. Evolution is the process that can lead us back to that state.

In the Gita this is not merely philosophy. Applied to our

daily lives, it becomes practical, compassionate psychology. Throughout nature all three gunas are constantly in play, with one or another predominant at any moment. Since body and mind are made of the same stuff, the gunas interact the same way within personality too. The Gita summarizes all this in a series of verses:

> It is the three gunas born of prakriti – sattva, rajas, and tamas – that bind the immortal Self to the body. Sattva – pure, luminous, and free from sorrow – binds us with attachment to happiness and wisdom. Rajas is passion, arising from selfish desire and attachment. These bind the Self with compulsive action. Tamas, born of ignorance, deludes all creatures through heedlessness, indolence, and sleep.
>
> Sattva predominates when rajas and tamas are transformed. Rajas prevails when sattva is weak and tamas overcome. Tamas prevails when rajas and sattva are dormant.
>
> When sattva predominates, the light of wisdom shines through every gate of the body. When rajas predominates, a person runs about pursuing selfish and greedy ends, driven by restlessness and desire. When tamas is dominant, a person lives in darkness – slothful, confused, and easily infatuated.
>
> (14:5–8, 10–13)

We can see the dynamics of this theory by looking at ourselves. When we want to be of some service to those around us, when we forgive, when we find it difficult to nourish resentments or to carry a grudge, sattva is coming into play. At the opposite pole is tamas: inertia, resistance. Everyone shows a streak of tamas when apathy starts its theme song: "Who cares? What does it matter? What does it matter if I finish this job? What does it matter if people get hurt? What does it matter if this isn't legal? What does it matter if the world explodes?" This is the vocabulary of tamas on the human level, and "I don't care" is its simplest form.

Tamas can show itself in other ways too. "This is too big a problem for me. This is too great a challenge. This world is too troubled for me to help; what can one person do?" Or simply, "I can't do this" – which often means no more than "I don't want to." Tamas predominates in a person who is apathetic, who is insensitive to the suffering around him and just cannot make much effort. It is the insidious voice that whispers, "Drop out. Quit your job. Turn your back. Run away." Tamas flourishes by paralyzing the will, the faculty we need most in personal growth.

In spiritual evolution, tamas is the aspect of mind that holds us back, and it will dog our progress at every level of consciousness. When we learn to deal with it on the physical level, it will retrench somewhere less obvious, such as procrastination, failure of the will, or paralysis when we have to do something we dislike. If we are doing our best in meditation, we will always be on the front lines of the struggle with tamas. Drowsiness in deeper meditation, for example, may be a sign that we have reached a frontier in consciousness and lack the will to push into unknown territory.

A mental block consists of tamas, and the human being has an unending series of such impediments at every level of consciousness. One familiar sign that we are nearing a mental block – something we have to work through because tamas is rising – is that we can't seem to get up in the morning. This is a warning that tamas is gaining ascendence. The way to press through that resistance is not to weigh pros and cons, which only makes tamas stronger, but to throw off the covers and give one leap out of bed. It seems a small step, but life consists of small moments, and each time we resist an impulse to do nothing, we are transforming that block of inertia into energy: that is, transforming tamas into rajas.

Rajas is dominant whenever we feel active, energetic, full of drive and enterprise or driven by passion. Rajas enables us to get things done, but it is also the glue of attachment that gets us caught in the pursuit of personal pleasure, profit, prestige, or power. Uncontrolled, rajas runs amok – and when it won't let us rest, rajas is crying out that it is ready to be transformed into sattva. In that highest state, we are energetic without being driven by time or self-centered attachments. Wherever we find someone calm, clear, and kind under pressure, compassionate in the face of provocation, we can be sure that sattva is predominant.

The Gita is giving us a precious secret here: how to transform the lower levels of consciousness into the highest, where forgiveness, forbearance, compassion, and love come into play. In nature, the gunas interact mindlessly, but as human beings we can draw on the will, the higher mind, to change them as we choose. We can draw upon rajas to transform tamas, and then channel and harness rajas to transform it into sattva. When sattva predominates, all the energies of life are in balance. This is not the unitive state that yoga aims at, but sattva is the platform we must reach in order to move beyond the gunas altogether into unitary consciousness.

We make this kind of progress only by degrees, but changes can be decisive. I remember a profile in the *New Yorker* of a man named Theodore Taylor who, upon graduating from college in physics, proved to be a brilliant designer of nuclear weapons. He was a gentle, peaceloving chap; he merely happened to have a genius for making bombs.

As a young physicist in the heady years following the Manhattan Project, Ted Taylor found himself tantalized by the challenge of ballistics problems no one else could solve. He simply couldn't allow a second-rate bomb design to lie around without improving on it, even when an "elegant solution" meant a smaller, simpler device that could kill more people. "The worst invention in physical history," he admitted, "was also the most interesting." And he added an illuminating observation: "The theorist's world is a world of the best people and the worst of possible results." That is what moha does, and it is the direct result of rajas.

But this was a sensitive man who quickly began to think about the consequences of his work. Soon after his first daughter was born – no coincidence, he said – he turned exclusively to peacetime uses of atomic energy, and after a while he began warning anyone who would listen about the implications of miniaturized atomic weapons – not a new danger, but in this case people knew the warning came from a man who knew precisely how easily such a weapon could be made. In his latter years, I learned, he devoted himself to alternative energy technologies and had begun studying the Gita and learning to meditate – a perfect illustration of how rajas can be transformed into sattva in this life.

In this sense, evolution is the transformation of energy from one state into another, the way the power in a rushing river is converted into electrical energy by a water mill. If we think of tamas as ice, rajas is the energy in that block of ice released into flowing water when it melts, and sattva is the same energy conserved and harnessed when water is turned to steam to drive a turbine. The differences are only of "name and form" – namarupa again. This is a reassuring way to classify humanity, because it implies that no one need be stuck in any of these states. Just as ice can always be made into water and water can always be turned into steam and harnessed, even the most tamasic individual can take up the spiritual life. It's an apt illustration, because an incredible amount of energy is released when tamas is transformed. I have seen young people crippled by inertia become powerhouses of creative activity through the practice of meditation.

In its native state, consciousness is a continuous flow of awareness. Creation is the fall from this state into fragmented, divided, sometimes stagnant awareness, which hides reality under the confused activity of the gunas. I like to think this is the significance of the Fall in the biblical account of creation. Eden is not a place but a state of consciousness, and the Fall is not an event that took place thousands of years ago but a process that is still continuing – about to hit bottom, perhaps, but still continuing. What we are trying to do in meditation is stop the fall and go back to Eden – reversing this decline by resolving fragmentation back into unity, not in the physical world but in our mode of seeing.

Roughly speaking, most of us have rajasic minds, which means we are thinking all the time, working all the time, without conscious control of what the mind is doing. That is rajas. The Gita would draw a distinction between conscious, voluntary, intentional thinking and mental activity that is involuntary, conditioned, and compulsive. In sattva, the workings of the mind come under conscious control, which means that most forms of unnecessary thinking – worrying, for example – simply disappear.

One of the most thrilling discoveries in sadhana is that we don't have to act on our states of mind. We don't even have to be affected by our states of mind. If we have negative thoughts – resentments, doubts, jealousies, fears – we don't have to act on any of them, and simply by not acting on negative thoughts, we start transforming the energy in them into sattva.

Rajas, then, is the ordinary mind, desiring, worrying, and resenting, scheming and competing, and getting more frustrated all the time. To the extent we are able to establish control over this, the mind becomes sattva. And the vast unconscious mind is tamas. It's just chaos. Most of us know how much clutter one person can accumulate in even a few years; our closets and garages bear witness. Imagine the amount of clutter your mind must have picked up in the course of a lifetime and multiply that over eons of lifetimes; that is the unconscious, the dumping-ground of evolution.

The picture that tamas presents at this level is so overwhelming that I will draw a veil over it, except to say that this is the repository of immense power – power that hides a limitless treasury of resources that flow into our hands when we discover that power and harness it. Until then, however, it is just darkness, the literal meaning of tamas.

The pull of tamas from these depths keeps us swinging like

a pendulum from guna to guna, unable to make lasting commitments or to be loyal. To give just one illustration, most people involved in selfless work have had someone come up and say with honest enthusiasm, "I want to help, and I have a lot of resources. Just tell me what you need." Then, after a week or two, the same person begins to find reservations and conditions. One month later, when you meet by chance, he will say sincerely, "You're doing such good work! I wish you every success."

The first of these instances is what the Gita calls sattvic giving, without any strings or expectations. The second is born of rajas: "Will you put my name on a plaque on the cornerstone, in beautiful calligraphy?" And the third, of course, is our old friend tamas. The Gita gives several such illustrations of how the gunas operate, and it is remarkably specific:

> Giving simply because it is right to give, without
> thought of return, at the proper time, in proper cir-
> cumstances, and to a worthy person, is sattvic giving.
> Giving with regrets or in the expectation of receiving
> some favor or of getting something in return is rajasic.
> Giving at an inappropriate time, in inappropriate
> circumstances, and to an unworthy person, without
> affection or respect, is tamasic. (17:20–22)

The way to steady the mind and transform these lower states into sattva is to stand firm in our highest resolutions and not let ourselves be pushed into acting on rajas or tamas. In this way, again, we are changing consciousness to be changeless – making the mind unshakable no matter what the forces and circumstances outside.

What is happening as we do this is fascinating: we are unifying consciousness by unifying our desires, which are expressions of rajas in a million different channels. Desire is energy, like electricity; it can be harnessed or be drained away. In the earlier stages of personal evolution, desire is often sluggish; tamas rules, locking up the energy required to reach for a better life. As rajas rises, desires arise and multiply. A great many people live in this middle stage, with so many desires that there is little power in any of them. Seeking countless trivial things, often concerning personal appearance or prestige, they lead superficial lives, rarely achieving success in any field.

As experience deals out its lessons, however – perhaps over lifetimes – such people begin to focus their desires. They learn that having many small desires cannot bring fulfillment: at best, small desires bring only small satisfactions, stirring the desire for something that abides.

Those who are born with relatively few desires, by contrast, stand out for leading outwardly successful lives. They have focused the power of desire enough to accomplish what matters most. And a fortunate few are born with just two or three desires. They are the geniuses, the great scientists, athletes, humanitarians, musicians, artists, writers, statesmen, who make their mark in whatever field they choose. In that field they have harnessed rajas, though often not in the rest of their lives. But among them are a few who have made their lives shine. They have learned to transform the whole of personality into sattva, making their lives a work of art.

Last – rarest and most precious – come a handful who are possessed by only one desire: the overriding need to know who they are and what life is for. Out of this group come the great mystics. They have tasted what life has to offer, sampled what they can achieve through personal ambition, and found it all too small to satisfy them. The longing for Self-realization has become so gargantuan that it has consumed every lesser desire – for pleasure, for profit, for prestige, for power – as a raging river assimilates the creeks that drain into it. In practical terms, this means that consciousness is very nearly unified: we are not pulled in different directions by competing forces; all our capacity to desire is focused on one end. Tamas and rajas are almost completely transformed, setting the stage for the unitive state.

Lifelong Learning

Another way to look on this progression appeals to me as an educator: this is lifelong learning, a long series of experiments and explorations in the laboratory of life in pursuit of Self-discovery.

We know what a struggle it is to understand a school

subject that seems alien. Tamas just blindfolds the intellect. In my case, I could look at the same theorem in geometry a thousand times and it would never reveal its secrets; each time was like the first. We can go through life like this, getting the same lessons over and over but unable to get it right. Often we don't even know we are being set a lesson. It's as if we had to read a language in an unknown script, or make sense of a message that we don't realize is in code.

On the other hand, everyone finds it a thrill to learn something difficult and master it. One year I came home with such poor marks in mathematics that I felt I was letting my family down by not giving it my best. I applied myself and passed with distinction – only to win the dubious distinction of being encouraged then to drop literature and become an engineer. That didn't tempt me for a moment, but I found it deeply satisfying to master a subject I had thought beyond my reach. Life can be like that too if we approach it in the same way: not asking "What can I get?" or "Why does this happen to me?" but "What can I learn from this? How can I learn to manage this better?"

Most of us start adult life under the impression that if we can make a lot of money, own a nice house, do things we like, and enjoy a reasonable measure of prestige in our chosen field, we are going to be satisfied. When we talk to people who have done these things, however, they often confide that what they wanted has slipped through their fingers. Christine and I had a friend in India who was given to building beautiful homes. She had money, good taste, and plenty of imagination, and when we met her she had just finished a new home, decorated it beautifully, and moved in expecting to be happy the rest of her life. After a year or two, she reached the realization that this wasn't going to happen after all. She moved out, went to another locality, and built another beautiful home in a different style, again under the honest impression that she could live there happily forever. This too turned out to be not quite what she was looking for; when we last saw her, she was moving on again to someplace new.

All of us do this, one way or another, and the Gita asks simply, "For how long? When will you tire of playing this game of seeking happiness outside? Don't you want to know who you are and what life is for?" In every country, there are a few people who have gone through the smorgasbord of life and are fed up. Making money, they decide, is child's play. Enjoying pleasure – where is the challenge? And as for fame, who wants a food that dead men eat? They have tried these things and found no meaning in them; now they want to know why they are here and whether life has any overriding purpose. Most important, they see that death is walking behind them, closer every day, and they have no idea what to do.

Fortunately, for people who are sensitive and have some capacity to learn from their experience, it takes only a little playing with pleasure and profit to conclude that such things cannot bring fulfillment. They are life's fast learners, and they save themselves a great deal of suffering. The rest of us go on playing the same game over and over and over without learning from it. We get caught in this search for happiness outside and cannot change.

But there comes a point of no return. A friend of ours who was an airline pilot told us that in his flying days, when crossing the ocean he had to keep his eye constantly on the gas supply because after a point there is not enough fuel to return. Similarly, there comes a point in life when retracing our steps becomes almost impossible. When we cannot change direction, when we have no choice but to continue playing with these finite things that we know cannot satisfy us, the Bhagavad Gita points out that so far as evolution is concerned, we have wasted our life.

According to the Gita, we have come into life to learn that nothing finite can satisfy us. In the Upanishads there is a quiet statement: "There is no joy in the finite; there is joy only in the Infinite." Anything that is limited, anything that comes and goes, anything that is personal or private or separate from the rest of life, will simply fail to satisfy us because our nature has no limits. All of us need a certain amount of experimentation to make this discovery, but the sooner we learn, the earlier we can avoid the frustration and sense of failure that comes as we chase one will-o'-the-wisp after another until life ebbs away. Our need for the Infinite is inscribed on every cell of our being, and we cannot rest until that need is fulfilled.

Interestingly, the name Krishna comes from the root *krish,* to draw or pull. There is a force in the depths of our consciousness that is operating all the time, trying to draw us in, but we are looking elsewhere. Life is constantly sending us reminders about where happiness is to be found, but we do not know the code. We think this force is coming from outside, so we run about seeking meaning anywhere but in our own heart.

How quickly we learn, of course, depends on us. People are different. Broadly, Sri Krishna says, there are four kinds of people who take up the spiritual life:

> Some come to the spiritual life because of suffering,
> some in order to understand life; some come through a
> desire to achieve life's purpose, and some come who are
> men and women of wisdom. (7:16)

Those who learn early and quickly, as I said, avoid a great deal of sorrow. Others need a good deal of experimentation before they understand. But most of us have to learn the hard way, through the suffering that comes when we pursue happiness as if we were separate from the rest of life. Pain makes us step back and take a long look at our way of living. That is its evolutionary purpose, and that is why it is the most effective teacher we can have.

Unfortunately, a good deal of pain may be required for

those who are unwilling to learn. But when we come to under-stand with our heart the role pain plays in life, we see there is no event, however tragic, from which we cannot learn and grow. I have often heard people say that if it had not been for a serious illness or accident, they would never have swerved from a destructive way of life.

This understanding does not come easily to anyone, but when you can keep it in mind at all times, you find that your locus of control moves gradually from the world outside to within yourself. You begin to feel you have control over your life. You are not a plaything of blind forces; you have a direc-tion to which you can refer circumstances, so that you are always able to make choices whatever comes – the choices by which we learn.

Self Against Self

In the Gita, the first of these choices is the criti-cal one: to turn inward. After that basic decision, many other choices, increasingly difficult, will follow when we are ready to learn. But until we make this first choice, the Gita says, "the decisions of life are many-branched and endless" (2:41).

And that brings us back to the war within, for every one of these choices involves a struggle between our higher and lower selves. The Gita spells out the secret of victory in two of my favorite verses, so simple and so profound:

Reshape yourself through the power of your will; never
let yourself be degraded by self-will. The will is the only
friend of the Self, and the will is the only enemy of the
Self.

To those who have conquered themselves, the will is
a friend. But it is the enemy of those who have not
found the Self within them. (6:5–6)

The word *atman* – literally, "self" – is used in more than
one sense here. The Atman is the divine spark that shines in
our consciousness, but in these verses, in a play on words,
"self" refers also to the higher mind – will, effort, judgment,
perseverance – as distinguished from the lower mind.
Krishna is telling Arjuna, "Always raise yourself by your own
self" – by the efforts of your higher self; by your real Self, the
Atman. Every day, raise yourself by strengthening your will
and reducing your self-will. Never allow yourself to demean
yourself; never do anything that will lower yourself. Raise
your higher self with the help of your lower self; never drag
your higher self down to the level of your lower. The divine
Self is pure, selfless, unstained; the lower self is selfish and
subject to whims and caprices, obsessed with getting its own
way. Anything that lowers human consciousness, therefore,
moves us backwards in evolution.

"Raise yourself by yourself." It has stern implications. If we
fall, Sri Krishna is implying, nobody has pushed us. We have

made ourselves fall. Every time we indulge our separateness, we are lowering ourselves, making it more difficult to raise ourselves by our own will. There is only one person who can degrade us, and that is we ourselves. Nobody else. And there is only one person who can help us to rise to our full stature; no one can do it for us.

Sri Krishna finds this statement so important that he repeats it. You have only one friend in the world, he says, your will; and you have only one enemy in the world, your will. Don't ever weaken your friend or strengthen your enemy by indulging in self-will, by getting angry, by putting your welfare ahead of those around you. Ultimately, our one lasting friend is the higher self, our will. If we weaken the will, we have no friend who can stand by us, no relative, no one to bond with anywhere. We don't have enemies outside, but we have the fiercest of enemies inside if we undermine our will.

These are sobering words, for they lay responsibility for our drawbacks and defects directly on our own shoulders. This is how we have made ourselves, Krishna implies, through the choices we have made in the past. But by that which we fall, we can rise. The same power that we have allowed to work against us can be transformed, so that we can draw upon it to raise ourselves to a higher level of consciousness. The choice lies in our hands.

Thus we find ourselves on the battlefield again, pulled by conflicting forces. In tamas there is no struggle, for struggle requires effort. In sattva too there is no struggle, because conflict has been transcended and harmony achieved. Rajas is the period of struggle, the "battlefield of dharma," where tamas and sattva fight over us until tamas is transformed and rajas harnessed.

But this is not the end, as those earlier verses hinted. Sattva is not the unitive state; it too is conditioning. Its role is to set the stage for going beyond the conditioning of the gunas completely:

> The wise see clearly that all action is the work of the
> gunas. Knowing that which is above the gunas, they
> enter into union with me. . . . They are unmoved by the
> harmony of sattva, the activity of rajas, or the delusion
> of tamas. They feel no aversion when these forces are
> active, nor do they crave for them when these forces
> subside. (14:19, 22)

To achieve this state, however, requires more than all the effort we can muster, more than the unification of all desires. As Sri Krishna will explain, it requires a power beyond personal agency entirely: the power that traditional religious language calls grace.

CHAPTER TWELVE

◇ *Into Battle*

WE HAVE COME a long way since the Gita began – covered, it seems, the whole field of space and time, the evolution of the universe since creation. Now it is time to return to the beginning: to Arjuna's crisis and the war within.

In the long ascent to perfection that is yoga, Shankara says, there are three blessings. The first is to be born as a human being. It has taken four to five billion years to acquire a name and a Social Security number – billions of years of evolution from primordial matter to matter that is very personal indeed. How much travail and tribulation have gone into the making of this human body, the necessary context for attaining Self-realization!

After lifetimes of experimentation as human beings, the Gita adds, we begin to see that nothing external can satisfy us. Then the second blessing arises: an intense desire to know who we really are. In every country and every religion, there have been people who cannot rest until they find the supreme reality within themselves. No particular country or religion should claim this exclusive privilege; but in India, for no reason I can give, there has been an unbroken succession of such men and women for more than five thousand years.

When this desire grows all-consuming, the third blessing comes: close association with someone who has been enabled to achieve Self-realization and can safely help others to attain it as well. For Arjuna, this turning point marks the real beginning of the Gita, when he appeals to Sri Krishna:

> My will is paralyzed, and I am utterly confused. Tell me
> which is the better path for me. Let me be your disciple.
> I have fallen at your feet; give me instruction. (2:7)

When we too reach this point, we have begun to take our evolution into our own hands. Like a salmon fighting its way upstream, we begin to struggle against the current of our conditioning and find our way to the headwaters of living in freedom.

Yet after years of struggle – even decades, perhaps even a lifetime – we reach a point where no amount of personal effort can take us further. However hard we try, we cannot complete the transformation of our deepest personal desires into universal ones – which means that a barrier of separateness, subtle but impenetrable, stands between us and our goal. This is the frontier between the personal unconscious, where the sense of "I" still rules, and the universal or collective unconscious – undifferentiated prakriti – in which there is no sense of individuality at all. We need to change to a level of consciousness where the personal self disappears, and we simply don't know how.

This should scarcely be surprising. After all, most of us have difficulties managing even on the conscious level. Where the subconscious is concerned, sometimes we manage and sometimes we don't. But where the unconscious is concerned, nobody has any say in it. When we see we are being challenged to regulate the unconscious, we want to quote Sam Goldwyn: "In two words, im-possible." Yet in every tradition there are mystics who will testify, "Yes, it is impossible, but we have done it." Compared with this, I don't think any earthly achievement can even be mentioned.

What is it like to walk in the unconscious? The individual observer simply isn't present there, and we have no language for describing that kind of experience. It is like holding something you cannot hold, seeing something you cannot see, hearing something you cannot hear – we have to fall back on poetry, on the language of Zen or the Sufi mystics or St. John of the Cross.

This is the most agonizing chapter in sadhana. We have come so far, given so much, devoted everything we can to this search; now every way forward seems blocked by an invisible wall. Stepping off the level of personal consciousness into the depths of the unknown requires something more than reason. It requires faith: faith that there is something awaiting us, faith that this is something we can actually do.

"Faith" is a problematic word here, because religious faith has become so badly confused with fanaticism and seems opposed to reason. In fact, what is meant here is poles apart from fanaticism and complements reason. "Faith" is an inadequate translation of the Sanskrit word *shraddha* – another of those important terms with no equivalent in any language I know of. Generally speaking, shraddha is the basis of how one looks at life. Here it means not just faith and beliefs but assumptions, conditioning, motivation, personal capacity, and the particular stage in evolution that one has reached, both individually and in the long arc of spiritual growth.

We depend on faith all the time in a million ways small and large throughout every day; we couldn't take a step without it. We show faith in physics whenever we cross a bridge, and faith in economics (of all things) when we accept slips of paper in exchange for goods or services. We show faith daily in doctors and medicines; we believe scientists who tell us absurd-sounding things about warped space and the first few seconds of creation and matter disappearing down holes in the sky; and of course we show all kinds of misplaced trust too, in politicians' promises and get-rich-quick schemes and the assurances of those who tell us what we want to believe about "wars to end war" and "energy too cheap to meter." The sum of what each of us believes tells a great deal about who we are. In fact, the Gita says, it is what we are. The Bible says the same thing: "As a man thinks in his heart, so he is." We are what we believe; we become what we believe – most critically in what we believe we are.

It follows that if we can change what we believe, we can change what we become – and thereby, if only a little, change the world around us.

Let me give some simple illustrations. In the village where I grew up, the monsoon rains bring hundreds of frogs to cluster around our temple pools at night and sing their throaty chorus. And every night during the monsoon season, particularly at nightfall, snakes come out – some of them huge – and try to catch a frog or two and swallow it alive. It was ghastly to listen to, and even as a little boy I wasn't able to sleep with those frogs crying for help and me unable to do anything. During the day, if I saw a big snake eyeing a frog and the frog looking at me with mute appeal as if to say, "Save me," I used to leave my friends and jump in to scare the snake away. My classmates laughed at me. "It's just going to come back again," they'd say. "Why should you take sides like that and deprive the snake of its food?" I didn't know how to answer, but my grandmother did: "It is a snake's dharma to kill. Your dharma is to save."

This is a very basic shraddha: the belief, deep below the surface level of consciousness, that we have come into life to give and not to hurt, to help and not to harm.

Everybody, including a little child, has shraddha. I don't think there is any human being who can function in life without shraddha. It can be wrong shraddha; then they function wrongly. It can be right shraddha; then they function rightly. But the message of the Gita is that if your shraddha is low, you can elevate it; if your shraddha is selfish, you can change it to selfless; if your shraddha is violent, you can make it nonviolent. To me this is the glory of the human being: not our technological accomplishments, no matter how laudable, but the fact that there is nobody who cannot change the meanest shraddha into something noble.

The word *shraddha* can be taken as meaning literally "that which is placed in the heart." To make a bad Sanskrit pun, for years my shraddha was *shiro-dha,* "that which is placed in the head": higher education. We all know that that which is placed in the head is often not of much significance in everyday life. This began to puzzle me even before I took to meditation. As a graduate student, whenever a famous author or scholar came to campus to speak I would be seated right in front to take in everything they said. But when they started taking questions, I'd suddenly realize that my unlettered grandmother could give much wiser answers. And that baffled me. Here were men and women with stellar educations, yet on topics like how to live they seemed so immature and misleading.

But my shraddha was that whatever is placed in your head is what you are. That's what I was building my life on. That's how I looked at life. Those were the people I respected; those were the people I wanted to emulate. Having spent sixteen or seventeen years undergoing all this brain-stuffing, it was shattering to take these idols off their pedestals and put them away in the attic with the old copies of *Punch* and broken toys.

Another example, this time dealing with something that seems impossible: ice skating. Coming from South India, I cannot take two steps on ice. I cannot take even one step; that would be the beginning and end of my skating. I have tried. In Minneapolis, when I first saw that ol' Mississippi River turn to ice, I couldn't believe it. I had read about such things, Hans Brinker and all that, but to me the dharma of a river was to flow. Here it had not just stopped flowing but turned solid, while even little children flew about on the surface dancing and twirling and doing impossible things.

Yet years later, when Christine and I took our nieces to a skating rink in California, I began to understand that any-body, even someone like me, could learn to skate if he or she just put in the effort. If I had been born in Minneapolis instead of South India, and spent my time on the skating rink instead of in rivers and on soccer fields, my "ice shraddha" would have been very different. I would have had faith that this is something that can be learned.

You can see this shraddha in champion athletes and per-formers: if you want something badly enough, you won't let anything come in the way. That's an elementary shraddha, but it illustrates the faith that intense desire can achieve impossible things.

Ice skating is a trivial example, but the point is far-reaching. I am old enough to remember when it was considered physiologically impossible for a human being to run a mile in less than four minutes. Virtually everyone believed this, while the world record crept closer and closer to an invisible barrier that could not be crossed – until Roger Banister came along with a different shraddha and turned in a time of three minutes and fifty-nine-plus seconds in 1954. Then the old shraddha of impossibility fell away. It takes very little to dismiss this kind of faith: just one person is enough.

The most important instance of shraddha, then, is the image we have of ourselves in our hearts – the paradigm of personality, if you like, which governs what we will seek in life, the purpose we will follow, the very basis of our pattern of living. The Gita sums it up quietly:

> Every creature is born with faith of some kind, either sattvic, rajasic, or tamasic. . . . Our faith conforms to our nature, Arjuna. Human nature is made of faith. A person is what his shraddha is. (17:2–3)

We are what our shraddha is – and since virtually all of us believe we are physical creatures, so we spend our lives seeking physical satisfaction. The challenge of the Gita is to slowly change our image of ourselves from wholly physical to essentially spiritual. It is when we start trying to do this in the depths of the unconscious that the real war within begins.

At this point there can be an impulse to run away by plunging into distracting activities and fresh entanglements. But – just as for Arjuna in this war – it's too late now to run away. We can take our time exploring any number of byways; they are all going to be blind alleys. Finally we realize there is only one thing to do: take it on. Your mind will assure you that you can't make it. Don't listen: that's not you; it's the voice of a ventriloquist, the ego, whose separateness is being threatened. If you couldn't make it, you would never have got this far.

But don't look for any shortcuts, any speedy solutions; there aren't any.

What does it mean to regulate the unconscious? Sri Krishna uses a significant word, *shanti,* for which "peace" is a very inadequate translation. Shanti is "the peace that passes understanding." It refers to a state of mind in which all desires are fulfilled, all conflicts resolved, and all fears banished. The practical significance is that once we reach this state, we can enter into the unconscious and bid any storm that is brewing there to be quiet. All thoughts can be quietened. We don't have to tell anger or fear or greed to be quiet; we just say, like Jesus in the storm, "Be still," and stillness reigns.

In my village school, when a teacher entered the room and said, "Children, be quiet," we were expected to stop whatever we were doing and give our full attention. But the unconscious is pandemonium. No teacher has ever been there; there is not even any school. We have to build the school, prescribe the curriculum, and then train the mind every day, just as if it were starting kindergarten. When I was small, we had to learn the multiplication tables up to times sixteen, not only forwards but backwards too. Just try doing that! We had to recite every evening after class or else we couldn't go home. No sophisticated educational psychology; we just learned. Training the unconscious is like that. When you go on repeating something over and over, it becomes natural. As Gandhi said, it requires the patience of someone trying to empty the sea with a cup – but it works. Finally, even if someone shakes you out of deep sleep in the middle of the night and says something rude, you won't be rude in return. Even in your most befuddled intellectual moods, love surges: you know you cannot hurt anyone; you know you cannot be unkind. You can't be taken unawares.

To do this, however, requires tremendous focus. All desires must be unified. Each of us has millions of little desires, and every desire has a certain force in it; it is the force of all these millions of little desires unified that enables you to open the door into the unconscious. When you have had a serious quarrel, for example, you know what happens when you try to read or watch a movie; the force of your anger scatters your attention to the winds. How do we deal with these unconscious hurricanes? Arjuna asks for us:

O Krishna, the stillness of divine union that you
describe is beyond my comprehension. How can the
mind, which is so restless, attain lasting peace? The
mind is restless, turbulent, powerful, violent; trying to
control it is like trying to tame the wind. (6:33–34)

In meditation, this is just what we are trying to do: turn a
hurricane around so that it blows in the opposite direction.
Beneath the conscious level, anger, fear, and selfish desire are
blowing constantly in every human being. But their action
isn't predetermined; they blow in the direction they do
because that is our conditioning. If these winds are turned
around, their energy is transformed. Anger raging in at a
hundred miles per hour will come out as compassion – still
blowing at a hundred miles per hour. Lust blasting in at a hundred miles per hour will come out as love for all. There is no
loss of power, but now it is beneficial rather than destructive.

Arjuna complains that this cannot be done. Krishna replies
that it can, if we only keep trying:

It is true that the mind is restless and difficult to control.
But it can be conquered, Arjuna, through regular practice and detachment. Those who lack self-control will
find it difficult to progress in meditation; but those who
are self-controlled, striving earnestly through the right
means, will attain the goal. (6:35–36)

Yet here, at the very end of the Gita, he confides that in the long view we have very little choice. Like Arjuna, we are there on the battlefield already:

> If you say in your self-will, "I will not fight this battle," your resolve will be useless; your own nature will drive you into it. (18:59)

It's a terrible verse. If we refuse to fight the battle of life, our own karma will drive us into it. If we refuse to walk against the wind of conditioning, if we don't like getting sand in our eyes, eventually our own nature will make us change direction. The consequences of our thought and actions – karma – will drive us forward. That's what sorrow does. If we avoid fighting what is selfish in us, the consequences build up – the consequences of violating dharma, of ignoring the unity of life. Sooner or later, the very weight of our suffering will force us finally to turn and walk against the wind because that is the only way to find refuge. Here, Sri Krishna is appealing, "Why not do this now? Why wait till you can hardly walk and the storm is raging around you?"

The word *moha,* delusion, comes up again in these verses. Even if we think we enjoy living in a fog of separateness, the upward surge of evolution will drive us on. Aren't there creatures in the depths of the ocean that will go after the faintest ray of light? That's how we are; we have to move towards the light. We may protest that darkness is comfortable and struggling is painful; why not just stay in the dark? None of that matters; our need is for the light. That is the force of one of the oldest prayers in the Upanishads:

> From the unreal, lead me to the real.
> From darkness, lead me to light.
> From death, lead me to immortality.

At the end, once this struggle is over and the war is won, you will look back and see that everything in your life from birth on – being born in such a family, in such a place, going to such a school, having this kind of teachers and that kind of friends, playing with the toys of life till your fingers are burned to the second knuckle and not letting go until everything you're trying to hold on to is swept away, and you want to get free so passionately that you will risk whatever it costs – when all that is past and you have reached your goal, you see that from the day you were born you were marked for Self-realization. You were born with that destiny; all of us are. So when we try to hold on to money, the market crashes: we're not supposed to get caught there. We cultivate a meaningful relationship and the object of our desire goes and joins the Peace Corps – well, we're meant for a vastly higher consummation. This goes on and on, heartbreak after heartbreak, until we learn to read the code. Only then can we understand that all this suffering is what enabled us to turn our backs on our personal happiness and live for the welfare of the whole – in which, of course, our own personal welfare is included.

But we have got to stake everything we have. We can't hold back even one little thing, however small:

> The Lord dwells in the heart of all creatures and whirls them around upon the wheel of maya. Run to him for refuge with all your strength, and peace profound will be yours through his grace.
>
> Be aware of me always, adore me, make every act an offering to me, and you shall come to me; this I promise, for you are dear to me. Abandon all supports and look to me for protection. I shall purify you from the sins of the past; do not grieve. (18:61–62, 65–66)

This is the hallmark of the Gita: complete self-reliance, no dependence on any support except the Self, the Lord within. As long as we try to prop ourselves up with possessions and people, we have no freedom, and the props are guaranteed to fail. Sooner or later we have to learn to rely on the Self alone.

Letting go like this requires a real leap of faith. Being cautious, businesslike people, we say, "Lord, please give me Self-realization first; then I promise I'll throw the props away." This is the real problem. Sri Krishna says, "That's not the way business is done here. You throw them away first and then we'll see." We say, "And then you promise?" And he smiles and says, "No promises." That's the test. You not only stand to lose the cash in hand but to lose the credit also. And for some reason not known to me, there comes a point where you just don't mind – where you give whatever the cost. That's why mystics all talk the language of love: even in romance, it is the mark of all-consuming love to stake everything on a chance of attaining the beloved.

I have to admit that in this transaction Sri Krishna stands to get a lemon. What have we really got to give away? Frustration, insecurity, frittering away time in shopping centers . . . there is really nothing to lose. But at the time it seems everything, and the purpose of having to stake everything we hold on to, if I may so put it, is to unify consciousness – to love "with all our heart and all our mind and all our spirit and all our strength" so that we let go of ourselves. This all-consuming passion is why the Gita praises bhakti yoga, the way of love, as the surest and swiftest path to Self-realization:

> Those who set their hearts on me and worship me with
> unfailing devotion and faith are more established in
> yoga. [For] hazardous and slow is the path to the
> Unrevealed, difficult for physical creatures to tread. But
> they for whom I am the supreme goal, who do all work
> renouncing self for me and meditate on me with single-
> hearted devotion, these I will swiftly rescue from the
> fragment's cycle of birth and death, for their
> consciousness has entered into me. (12:2, 5–7)

I ask myself why Sri Krishna thrills every fiber of my being. It is not only during the day that my mind clings to him, but even when I am sound asleep. In the Hindu tradition, this is the concept of the Ishta or "chosen ideal": the form of God that answers to the heart's deepest desire. I mentioned earlier how diverse the Hindu tradition seems in its unity: my grandmother had her vision of God as Rama; for my mother it was Shiva; for me it is Krishna – the same truth, the same divinity, revealed in different ways in response to deep needs which can be completely fulfilled only by a particular personality of the Godhead. When love for this supreme ideal has consumed every personal desire in the heart, Self-realization is only a matter of time.

⊷

The Gita is nearly over now. Too soon, this sublime dialogue will end and Sri Krishna and Arjuna will be swept up in the rush of war. These may be the last moments they have together as teacher and student. Sri Krishna closes with a tender appeal:

> I give you these precious words of wisdom; reflect on
> them and then do as you choose. These are the last
> words I shall speak to you, dear one, for your spiritual
> fulfillment. You are very dear to me. (18:63–64)

Here we see the real appeal of the Bhagavad Gita. Krishna says, "I have given you the secret of living in health, happiness, love, and wisdom. Now reflect over it. Test it. Test it everywhere, in every situation. Then do what you think best." This is the Gita at its greatest. Sri Krishna doesn't say, "If you don't do this, you are going to be in hell for a trillion years." He is paying us the highest tribute: no threats, no intimidation, complete respect. "You are rational people, you are human beings, you know what is good and what is bad. I have shown you both sides, the path that leads to separateness, turmoil, and confusion and the path to happiness, love, and wisdom. Now choose."

And Arjuna, ever the warrior, rises to the challenge:

You have dispelled my doubts and delusions, and I
understand through your grace. My faith is firm now,
and I will do your will. (18:73)

EPILOGUE

SRI KRISHNA'S INSTRUCTION *to Arjuna is over now. It is past dawn on the battlefield; the war is about to begin. Sanjaya expresses his thrill at what he has heard:*

> *This is the dialogue I heard between Krishna and Arjuna, and the wonder of it makes my hair stand on end! Through divine grace, I have heard the supreme secret of spiritual union directly from the Lord of Yoga himself. Whenever I remember these wonderful, holy words, I am filled with joy. Wherever Krishna and Arjuna are together, there will be prosperity, happiness, and victory; of this I have no doubt. (18:74–76, 78)*

It is significant that the Gita doesn't end with victory, but with the resolution to fight till the war is won. This is the real promise of the Gita. "Wherever Krishna and Arjuna are together" – that is, whenever we model our lives on that of Arjuna; whenever we cultivate this kind of devoted relationship with our real Self, which is divine – however fierce the obstacles we face, victory is assured; and all along the way, our lives will grow in beauty. Mahatma Gandhi expressed it beautifully: "Full effort is full victory."

◈ *A Garland of Verses*

Selections from the Bhagavad Gita
translated by Eknath Easwaran

DHRITARASHTRA:

Tell me, Sanjaya, what is happening on the field of
battle, the field of dharma, where my army and my
enemies have gathered for war.

SANJAYA:

Standing between the two armies, Arjuna saw fathers
and grandfathers, teachers, uncles, and brothers, sons
and grandsons, in-laws and friends. Seeing his
kinsmen arrayed against him, Arjuna was overcome
by sorrow. Despairing, he spoke these words:

ARJUNA:

O Krishna, I see my own relations here anxious to
fight, and I am unable to stand; my mind seems to be
whirling. My will is paralyzed, and I am utterly
confused. Tell me which is the better path for me. Let

me be your disciple. I have fallen at your feet; give me
instruction.

KRISHNA:

You speak sincerely, but your sorrow has no cause. The
wise grieve neither for the living nor for the dead.
There has never been a time when you and I and the
kings gathered here have not existed, nor will there be
a time when we will cease to exist. As the same person
inhabits the body through childhood, youth, and old
age, so too at the time of death he attains another body.
The wise are not deluded by these changes.

The impermanent has no reality; reality lies in the
eternal. Those who have seen the boundary between
these two have attained the end of all knowledge.
Realize that which pervades the universe and is
indestructible; no power can affect this unchanging,
imperishable reality. The body is mortal, but that
which dwells in the body is immortal and
immeasurable.

One believes he is the slayer, another believes he is the
slain. Both are ignorant; there is neither slayer nor
slain. You were never born; you will never die. You
have never changed; you can never change. Unborn,
eternal, immutable, immemorial, you do not die when
the body dies. Realizing that which is indestructible,

eternal, unborn, and unchanging, how can you slay or
cause another to slay?

As one abandons worn-out clothes and acquires new
ones, so when the body is worn out a new one is
acquired by the Self, who lives within. The Self cannot
be pierced by weapons or burned by fire; water cannot
wet it, nor can the wind dry it. The Self cannot be
pierced or burned, made wet or dry. It is everlasting
and infinite, standing on the motionless foundations
of eternity. The Self is unmanifested, beyond all
thought, beyond all change. Knowing this, you should
not grieve. Death is inevitable for the living; birth is
inevitable for the dead. Since these are unavoidable,
you should not sorrow. Every creature is unmanifested
at first and then attains manifestation. When its end
has come, it once again becomes unmanifested. What
is there to lament in this? The Self of all beings, living
within the body, is eternal and cannot be harmed.
Therefore, do not grieve.

You have heard the intellectual explanation of sankhya,
Arjuna; now listen to the principles of yoga. By
practicing these you can break through the bonds of
karma. On this path effort never goes to waste, and
there is no failure. Even a little effort toward spiritual
awareness will protect you from the greatest fear.

Those who follow this path, resolving deep within themselves to seek me alone, attain singleness of purpose. For those who lack resolution, the decisions of life are many-branched and endless.

You have the right to work, but never to the fruit of work. You should never engage in action for the sake of reward, nor should you long for inaction. Perform work in this world, Arjuna, as a man established within himself – without selfish attachments, and alike in success and defeat. For yoga is perfect evenness of mind.

ARJUNA:

Tell me of those who live established in wisdom, ever aware of the Self, O Krishna. How do they talk? How sit? How move about?

KRISHNA:

They live in wisdom who see themselves in all and all in them, who have renounced every selfish desire and sense craving tormenting the heart. Neither agitated by grief nor hankering after pleasure, they live free from lust and fear and anger. Established in meditation, they are truly wise. Fettered no more by selfish attachments, they are neither elated by good fortune nor depressed by bad. Such are the seers.

Even as a tortoise draws in its limbs, the wise can draw in their senses at will. Aspirants abstain from sense pleasures, but they still crave for them. These cravings all disappear when they see the highest goal. Even of those who tread the path, the stormy senses can sweep off the mind. They live in wisdom who subdue their senses and keep their minds ever absorbed in me.

When you keep thinking about sense objects, attachment comes. Attachment breeds desire, the lust of possession that burns to anger. Anger clouds the judgment; you can no longer learn from past mistakes. Lost is the power to choose between what is wise and what is unwise, and your life is utter waste. But when you move amidst the world of sense, free from attachment and aversion alike, there comes the peace in which all sorrows end, and you live in the wisdom of the Self.

The disunited mind is far from wise; how can it meditate? How be at peace? When you know no peace, how can you know joy? When you let your mind follow the call of the senses, they carry away your better judgment as storms drive a boat off its charted course on the sea.

Use all your power to free the senses from attachment and aversion alike, and live in the full wisdom of the

Self. Such a sage awakes to light in the night of all
creatures. That which the world calls day is the night
of ignorance to the wise.

As rivers flow into the ocean but cannot make the vast
ocean overflow, so flow the streams of the sense-world
into the sea of peace that is the sage. But this is not so
with the desirer of desires.

They are forever free who renounce all selfish desires
and break away from the ego-cage of "I," "me," and
"mine" to be united with the Lord. This is the supreme
state. Attain to this, and pass from death to immortality.

ARJUNA:

What is the force that binds us to selfish deeds, O
Krishna? What power moves us, even against our will,
as if forcing us?

KRISHNA:

It is selfish desire and anger, arising from the guna of
rajas; these are the appetites and evils which threaten a
person in this life. Just as a fire is covered by smoke
and a mirror is obscured by dust, just as the embryo
rests deep within the womb, knowledge is hidden by
selfish desire – hidden, Arjuna, by this unquenchable
fire for self-satisfaction, the inveterate enemy of the
wise.

Selfish desire is found in the senses, mind, and intellect, misleading them and burying the understanding in delusion. Fight with all your strength, Arjuna! Controlling your senses, conquer your enemy, the destroyer of knowledge and realization.

The senses are higher than the body, the mind higher than the senses; above the mind is the intellect, and above the intellect is the Atman. Thus, knowing that which is supreme, let the Atman rule the ego, and slay the fierce enemy that is selfish desire.

I am the Lord who dwells in every creature. Through the power of my own maya, I manifest myself in a finite form. Whenever dharma declines and the purpose of life is forgotten, I manifest myself on earth. I am born in every age to protect the good, to destroy evil, and to reestablish dharma. As they approach me, so I receive them. All paths, Arjuna, lead to me.

Reshape yourself through the power of your will; never let yourself be degraded by self-will. The will is the only friend of the Self, and the will is the only enemy of the Self. To those who have conquered themselves, the will is a friend. But it is the enemy of those who have not found the Self within them.

Those who aspire to the state of yoga should seek the Self in inner solitude through meditation. With body and mind controlled they should constantly practice one-pointedness, free from expectations and attachment to material possessions.

Select a clean spot, neither too high nor too low, and seat yourself firmly on a cloth, a deerskin, and kusha grass. Then, once seated, strive to still your thoughts. Make your mind one-pointed in meditation, and your heart will be purified. Hold your body, head, and neck firmly in a straight line, and keep your eyes from wandering. With all fears dissolved in the peace of the Self and all actions dedicated to Brahman, controlling the mind and fixing it on me, sit in meditation with me as your only goal. Arjuna, those who eat too much or eat too little, who sleep too much or sleep too little, will not succeed in meditation. But those who are temperate in eating and sleeping, work and recreation, will come to the end of sorrow through meditation. Through constant effort they learn to withdraw the mind from selfish cravings and absorb it in the Self. Thus they attain the state of union.

When meditation is mastered, the mind is unwavering like the flame of a lamp in a windless place. In the still mind, in the depths of meditation, the Self reveals itself. Beholding the Self by means of the Self, an aspirant knows the joy and peace of complete fulfillment. Having attained that abiding joy beyond the senses, revealed in the stilled mind, they never swerve from the eternal truth. They desire nothing else and cannot be shaken by the heaviest burden of sorrow.

The practice of meditation frees one from all affliction. This is the path of yoga. Follow it with determination and sustained enthusiasm. Renouncing wholeheartedly all selfish desires and expectations, use your will to control the senses. Little by little, through patience and repeated effort, the mind will become stilled in the Self. Wherever the mind wanders, restless and diffuse in its search for satisfaction without, lead it within; train it to rest in the Self.

Abiding joy comes to those who still the mind. Freeing themselves from the taint of self-will, with their consciousness unified, they become one with Brahman. They see the Self in every creature and all creation in the Self. With consciousness unified through meditation, they see everything with an equal eye.

I am ever present to those who have realized me in every creature. Seeing all life as my manifestation, they are never separated from me. They worship me in the hearts of all, and all their actions proceed from me. Wherever they may live, they abide in me. When a person responds to the joys and sorrows of others as if they were his own, he has attained the highest state of spiritual union.

ARJUNA:

O Krishna, the stillness of divine union which you describe is beyond my comprehension. How can the mind, which is so restless, attain lasting peace? Krishna, the mind is restless, turbulent, powerful, violent; trying to control it is like trying to tame the wind.

KRISHNA:

It is true that the mind is restless and difficult to control. But it can be conquered, Arjuna, through regular practice and detachment.

Those who lack self-control will find it difficult to progress in meditation; but those who are self-controlled, striving earnestly through the right means, will attain the goal.

ARJUNA:

Krishna, what happens to one who has faith but who lacks self-control and wanders from the path, not attaining success in yoga? If one becomes deluded on the spiritual path, will he lose both worlds, like a cloud scattered in the sky? Krishna, you can dispel all doubts; remove this doubt which binds me.

KRISHNA:

Arjuna, my son, such a person will not be destroyed. When such people die, they are reborn into a home which is pure and prosperous. Or they may be born into a family where meditation is practiced; to be born into such a family is extremely rare. The wisdom they have acquired in previous lives will be reawakened, Arjuna, and they will strive even harder for Self-realization. Indeed, they will be driven on by the strength of their past disciplines. Even one who inquires after the practice of meditation rises above those who simply perform rituals. Through constant effort over many lifetimes, a person becomes purified of all selfish desires and attains the supreme goal of life.

Beyond this I have another, higher nature, Arjuna; it supports the whole universe and is the source of life in all beings. In these two aspects of my nature is the womb of all creation. The birth and dissolution of the cosmos itself take place in me. There is nothing that exists separate from me, Arjuna. The entire universe is suspended from me as my necklace of jewels.

In those who are strong, I am strength, free from passion and selfish attachment. I am desire itself, if that desire is in harmony with the purpose of life. The states of sattva, rajas, and tamas come from me, but I am not in them. These three gunas deceive the world: people fail to look beyond them to me, supreme and imperishable. The three gunas make up my divine maya, difficult to overcome. But they cross over this maya who take refuge in me.

Good people come to worship me for different reasons. Some come to the spiritual life because of suffering, some in order to understand life; some come through a desire to achieve life's purpose, and some come who are men and women of wisdom. When a person is devoted to something with complete faith, I unify his faith in that. Then, when faith is completely unified, one gains the object of devotion. In this way, every desire is fulfilled by me. Those whose understanding is small attain only transient satisfaction: those who worship the gods go to the gods. But my devotees come to me.

Few see through the veil of maya. The world, deluded, does not know that I am without birth and changeless. Delusion arises from the duality of attraction and aversion, Arjuna; every creature is deluded by these from birth. But those who have freed themselves from all wrongdoing are firmly established in worship of me. Their actions are pure, and they are free from the delusion caused by the pairs of opposites.

Those who remember me at the time of death will come to me. Do not doubt this. Whatever occupies the mind at the time of death determines the destination of the dying; always they will tend toward that state of being. Therefore, remember me at all times and fight on. With your heart and mind intent on me, you will surely come to me.

When you make your mind one-pointed through regular practice of meditation, you will find the supreme glory of the Lord. The Lord is the supreme poet, the first cause, the sovereign ruler, subtler than the tiniest particle, the support of all, inconceivable, bright as the sun, beyond darkness. Remembering him in this way at the time of death, through devotion and the power of meditation, with your mind completely stilled and your concentration fixed in the center of spiritual awareness between the eyebrows, you will realize the supreme Lord.

Remembering me at the time of death, close down the doors of the senses and place the mind in the heart. Then, while absorbed in meditation, focus all energy upwards to the head. Repeating in this state the divine name, the syllable *Om* that represents the changeless Brahman, you will go forth from the body and attain the supreme goal. I am easily attained by the person who always remembers me and is attached to nothing else. Such a person is a true yogi, Arjuna.

Those who realize life's supreme goal know that I am unmanifested and unchanging. Having come home to me, they are never separate again.

I pervade the entire universe in my unmanifested form. All creatures find their existence in me, but I am not limited by them. Behold my divine mystery! These creatures do not really dwell in me, and though I bring them forth and support them, I am not confined within them. They move in me as the winds move in every direction in space.

Those who worship me and meditate on me constantly, without any other thought – I will provide for all their needs. Whatever I am offered in devotion – a leaf, a flower, fruit, or water – I will accept as the loving gift of a dedicated heart. Whatever you do, make it an offering to me – the food you eat, the sacrifices you make, the help you give, even your suffering. In this way you will be freed from the bondage of karma, and from its results both pleasant and painful. Then, firm in renunciation and yoga, with your heart free, you will come to me.

I look upon all creatures equally; none are less dear to me and none more dear. But those who worship me with all their heart live in me, and I come to life in them. Even sinners become holy when they take refuge in me alone. Quickly their souls conform to dharma and they attain to boundless peace. Never forget this, Arjuna: no one who is devoted to me will ever come to harm.

All those who take refuge in me, whatever their birth, race, sex, or caste, will attain the supreme goal; this realization can be attained even by those whom society scorns. Kings and sages too seek this goal with devotion. Therefore, having been born in this transient and forlorn world, give all your love to me. Fill your mind with me; love me; serve me; worship me always. Seeking me in your heart, you will at last be united with me. To those steadfast in love and devotion I give spiritual wisdom, so that they may come to me. Out of compassion I destroy the darkness of their ignorance. From within them I light the lamp of wisdom and dispel all darkness from their lives.

I am the true Self in the heart of every creature, Arjuna, and the beginning, middle, and end of their existence. Among the shining gods I am Vishnu; of luminaries I am the sun; among the storm gods I am Marichi, and in the night sky I am the moon. Among the senses I am the mind, and in living beings I am consciousness. Among bodies of water I am the ocean, and among words, the syllable Om; I am the repetition of the holy name, and among mountains I am the Himalayas. I am death, which overcomes all, and the source of all beings still to be born. I am the feminine qualities: fame, beauty, perfect speech, memory, intelligence, loyalty, and forgiveness. I am the gambling of the gambler and the radiance in all that shines. I am effort, I am victory, and I am the goodness of the virtuous, the quality of sattva. I am the silence of the unknown and the wisdom of the wise. Wherever you find strength, or beauty, or spiritual power, you may be sure that these have sprung from a spark of my essence. But of what use is it to you to know all this, Arjuna? Just remember that I am, and that I support the entire cosmos with only a fragment of my being.

ARJUNA:
O Lord, master of yoga, if you think me strong enough to behold it, show me your immortal Self.

KRISHNA:

These things cannot be seen with your physical eyes;
therefore I give you spiritual vision to perceive my
form as the Lord of creation.

SANJAYA:

Having spoken these words, Krishna, the master of
yoga, revealed to Arjuna his most exalted form. If a
thousand suns were to rise in the heavens at the same
time, the blaze of their light would resemble the
splendor of that supreme spirit.

ARJUNA:

O Lord, I see within your body all the gods and every
kind of living creature. You are the supreme,
changeless Reality, the one thing to be known. You are
the refuge of all creation, the immortal spirit, the
eternal guardian of eternal dharma. You are without
beginning, middle, or end; you touch everything with
your infinite power. The sun and moon are your eyes,
and your mouth is fire; your radiance warms the
cosmos. O Lord, your presence fills the heavens and
the earth and reaches in every direction. I see the
three worlds trembling before this vision of your
wonderful and terrible form. As rivers flow into the
ocean, all the warriors of this world are passing into

your fiery jaws; all creatures rush to their destruction like moths into a flame. Filled with your terrible radiance, O Vishnu, the whole of creation bursts into flames. Tell me who you are, O Lord of terrible form. I bow before you; have mercy! I want to know who you are, you who existed before all creation. Your nature and workings confound me.

KRISHNA:

I am time, the destroyer of all; I have come to consume the world. Even without your participation, all the warriors gathered here will die.

SANJAYA:

Having heard these words, Arjuna trembled in fear. With joined palms he bowed before Krishna and addressed him stammering.

ARJUNA:

O Lord, you are the eternal spirit, who existed before the Creator and who will never cease to be. Lord of the gods, you are the abode of the universe. Changeless, you are what is and what is not, and beyond the duality of existence and nonexistence. Sometimes, because we were friends, I rashly said, "O, Krishna! Say, friend!" – casual, careless remarks. Whatever I may have said lightly, whether we were playing or resting, alone or in company, sitting together or eating, if it was disrespectful, forgive me for it, O Krishna. I did not know the greatness of your nature, unchanging and imperishable. O gracious Lord, I prostrate myself before you and ask for your blessing. As a father forgives his son, or a friend a friend, or a lover his beloved, so should you forgive me.

Of those who love you as the Lord of Love and those who seek you as the eternal, formless reality, whose way to you is sure and swift, love or knowledge?

KRISHNA:
For those who set their hearts on me and worship me with unfailing devotion and faith, the way of love leads sure and swift to me.

As for those who seek the transcendental Reality, without name, without form, contemplating the Unmanifested beyond the reach of thought and of feeling, with their senses subdued and mind serene and striving for the good of all beings, they too will verily come unto me. Yet hazardous and slow is the path to the Unrevealed, difficult for physical creatures to tread. But they for whom I am the supreme goal, who do all work renouncing self for me and meditate on me with single-hearted devotion, these I will swiftly rescue from the fragment's cycle of birth and death, for their consciousness has entered into me.

Still your mind in me, still your intellect in me, and
without doubt you will be united with me forever. If
you cannot still your mind in me, learn to do so
through the regular practice of meditation. If you lack
the will for such self-discipline, engage yourself in my
work, for selfless service can lead you at last to me. If
you are unable to do even this, surrender yourself to
me, disciplining yourself and renouncing the results of
all your actions. Better indeed is knowledge than
mechanical practice. Better than knowledge is
meditation. But better still is surrender of attachment
to results, because there follows immediate peace.

That one I love who is incapable of ill will, who is
friendly and compassionate. Living beyond the reach
of I and mine and of pleasure and pain, patient,
contented, self-controlled, firm in faith, with all their
heart and all their mind given to me – with such as
these I am in love. Not agitating the world or by it
agitated, they stand above the sway of elation,
competition, and fear: that one is my beloved.

They are detached, pure, efficient, impartial, never
anxious, selfless in all their undertakings; they are my
devotees, very dear to me. That one is dear to me who
runs not after the pleasant or away from the painful,

grieves not, lusts not, but lets things come and go as they happen.

That devotee who looks upon friend and foe with equal regard, who is not buoyed up by praise nor cast down by blame, alike in heat and cold, pleasure and pain, free from selfish attachments, the same in honor and dishonor, quiet, ever full, in harmony everywhere, firm in faith – such a one is dear to me.

The body is called a field, Arjuna; he who knows it is called the Knower of the field. I am the Knower of the field in everyone, Arjuna. Knowledge of the field and its Knower is true knowledge.

The field, Arjuna, is made up of the following: the five areas of sense perception; the five elements; the five sense organs and the five organs of action; the three components of the mind; and the undifferentiated energy from which all these evolved. In this field arise desire and aversion, pleasure and pain, the body, intelligence, and will. Whatever exists, Arjuna, animate or inanimate, is born through the union of the field and its Knower.

They alone see truly who see the Lord the same in every creature, who see the Deathless in the hearts of all that die. Seeing the same Lord everywhere, they do no harm to themselves or others. Thus they attain the supreme goal.

They alone see truly who see that all actions are performed by prakriti while the Self remains unmoved. When they see the variety of creation rooted in that unity and growing out of it, they attain fulfillment in Brahman.

This supreme Self is without a beginning, undifferentiated, deathless. Though it dwells in the body, Arjuna, it neither acts nor is touched by action. As space pervades the cosmos but remains unstained, the Self can never be tainted though it dwells in every creature. As the sun lights up the world, the Self dwelling in the field is the source of all light in the field. Those who, with the eye of wisdom, distinguish the field from its Knower and the way to freedom from the bondage of prakriti, attain the supreme goal.

ARJUNA:
What are the characteristics of those who have gone beyond the gunas, O Lord? How do they act? How have they passed beyond the gunas' hold?

KRISHNA:
They are unmoved by the harmony of sattva, the activity of rajas, or the delusion of tamas. They feel no

aversion when these forces are active, nor do they crave for them when these forces subside. Alike in honor and dishonor, alike to friend and foe, they have given up every selfish pursuit. Such are those who have gone beyond the gunas.

Neither the sun nor the moon nor fire can add to that light. This is my supreme abode, and those who enter there do not return to separate existence.

An eternal part of me enters into the world, assuming the powers of action and perception and a mind made of prakriti. When the divine Self enters and leaves a body, it takes these along as the wind carries a scent from place to place.

In this world there are two orders of being: the perishable, separate creature and the changeless spirit. But beyond these there is another, the supreme Self, the eternal Lord, who enters into the entire cosmos and supports it from within. I am that supreme Self, praised by the scriptures as beyond the changing and the changeless.

Every creature is born with faith of some kind, either sattvic, rajasic, or tamasic. Our faith conforms to our nature, Arjuna. Human nature is made of faith. A person is what his shraddha is.

Now listen, Arjuna: there are also three kinds of happiness. By sustained effort, one comes to the end of sorrow. That which seems like poison at first, but tastes like nectar in the end – this is the joy of sattva, born of a mind at peace with itself. Pleasure from the senses seems like nectar at first, but it is bitter as poison in the end. This is the kind of happiness that comes to the rajasic. Those who are tamasic draw their pleasures from sleep, indolence, and intoxication. Both in the beginning and in the end, this happiness is a delusion.

Listen, and I shall explain now, Arjuna, how those who have attained perfection attain Brahman, the supreme consummation of wisdom. Unerring in discrimination, sovereign of the senses and passions, free from the clamor of likes and dislikes, they lead a simple, self-reliant life based on meditation, controlling their speech, body, and mind. Free from self-will, aggressiveness, arrogance, anger, and the lust to possess people or things, they are at peace with themselves and others and enter into the unitive state. United with Brahman, ever joyful, beyond the reach of desire and sorrow, they have equal regard for every living creature and attain supreme devotion to me. By loving me they come to know me truly; they know my glory and enter into my boundless being. All their acts

are performed in my service, and through my grace
they win eternal life.

Make every act an offering to me; regard me as your
only protector. Make every thought an offering to me;
meditate on me always. Remembering me, you shall
overcome all difficulties through my grace. But if you
will not heed me in your self-will, nothing will avail
you. If you say, "I will not fight this battle," your
resolve will be useless; your own nature will drive you
into it. If you refuse to fight the battle of life, your own
karma will drive you into it.

The Lord dwells in the heart of every creature and
whirls them around upon the wheel of maya. Run to
him for refuge with all your strength, and peace
profound will be yours through his grace.

I give you these precious words of wisdom; reflect on
them and then do as you choose. These are the last
words I shall speak to you, dear one, for your spiritual
fulfillment. Be aware of me always, adore me, make
every act an offering to me, and you shall come to me;
this I promise, for you are dear to me. Abandon all
supports and look to me for protection. I shall purify
you from the sins of the past; do not grieve.

Have you listened with attention? Are you now free from your doubts and confusion?

ARJUNA:
You have dispelled my doubts and delusions, and I understand through your grace. My faith is firm now, and I will do your will.

◇ *Further Reading*

Eknath Easwaran. *The Bhagavad Gita.* 2nd ed. Classics
of Indian Spirituality. Tomales, Calif.: Nilgiri Press, 2007.
Translation and introduction by Eknath Easwaran with chapter
introductions and notes by Diana Morrison.

—— *The Upanishads.* 2nd ed. Classics of Indian Spirituality.
Tomales, Calif.: Nilgiri Press, 2007. The source texts of
Indian mysticism; translation and introduction by Eknath
Easwaran with notes and a concluding essay, "How to Read the
Upanishads", by Michael N. Nagler.

—— *The Bhagavad Gita for Daily Living.* 3 vols. Tomales,
Calif.: Nilgiri Press, 2020. A practical verse-by-verse
commentary presenting the Gita as a guide for those trying to
lead a spiritual life today. Includes Sanskrit text, translation,
and a separate introduction for each volume.

—— *Passage Meditation – A Complete Spiritual Practice.*
Tomales, Calif.: Nilgiri Press, 2016. First published 1978 as
Meditation. Describes the method of meditation referred to in
this book, inspired by chapter 6 of the Bhagavad Gita.

Huxley, Aldous. *The Perennial Philosophy.* Harper Perennial Modern Classics. N.Y.: Harper, 2004. First published 1945. The book that brought the phrase "perennial philosophy" into current use; includes many quotations from the world's great scriptures and mystics to illustrate how the key ideas of world mysticism have sprung up again and again in various cultures throughout history.

Prabhavananda, Swami. *The Spiritual Heritage of India.* Hollywood, Calif.: Vedanta Press, 1979. First published 1963 by Doubleday. An authoritative summary of Indian spirituality from its wellsprings through later developments, including Yoga and Buddhism.

Radhakrishnan, Sarvepalli. *The Bhagavadgita.* London: Allen & Unwin, 1948. A reliable scholarly translation with romanized Sanskrit text, notes, and a remarkably full introduction.

Sargeant, Winthrop. *The Bhagavad Gita.* SUNY Series in Cultural Perspectives. 25th anniversary edition. Albany, N.Y.: Excelsior Editions, State University of New York Press, 2009. Ed. Christopher Key Chapple; foreword by Huston Smith. A literal interlinear translation with parsed Sanskrit in Devanagari and roman transliteration for those who want to get close to the original text.

◈ Glossary

adhyaropa Superimposition. Though this term is not found in
   the Gita itself, it was used by the Vedantic philosopher
   Shankara in his commentary on the Gita. He defines it
   as the "apparent presentation [to consciousness] by way
   of remembrance of something previously perceived in
   something else." The usual example given is the mistake
   of superimposing the memory of a snake on a rope, for
   example at twilight when one can't see clearly that it is a
   rope.

ahamkara [*aham* "I"; *kara* "maker"] Self-will, separateness.

Arjuna One of the five Pandava brothers, a skilled warrior in
   Indian epic and legend. He is Sri Krishna's beloved disciple
   and friend in the Bhagavad Gita.

Atman "Self"; the innermost eternal soul in every creature.
   Occasionally, "oneself" in the ordinary sense.

avatar [Sanskrit *avatara*] The manifestation of God on earth, an
   earthly form of a divine being. From a root meaning "to
   cross down," the word connotes the descent of a divine
   being to earth for the welfare of the world. In the Gita
   Sri Krishna says, "Whenever dharma declines and the
   purpose of life is forgotten, I manifest myself on earth. I

am born in every age to protect the good, to destroy evil, and to reestablish dharma." (4:7-8)

avidya [*a* "not"; *vidya* "wisdom"] Ignorance, lack of wisdom. This term does not appear in the Gita, but is extremely important in later philosophical systems. The Gita, however, is very fond of all forms of the ancient verb *vid*, "to know," which is cognate with English words like "wisdom."

Bhagavad Gita [*Bhagavad* "lord"; *gita* "song"] "The Song of the Lord," name of a Hindu scripture that contains the instructions of Sri Krishna to Arjuna. It is one of the three key texts of Vedanta philosophy, along with the *Vedanta Sutras* and the Upanishads.

bhaya Fear. Many times the Gita warns that fear is a major obstacle to wisdom, and Krishna praises those who are free from it. "Not agitating the world or by it agitated, they stand above the sway of elation, competition, and fear: that one is my beloved." (12:15)

bhakti Devotion, worship, love of God.

bhakti yoga The way of love. One of the major paths to Self-realization in the Gita.

brahmavidya The science of knowing Brahman, the knowledge of reality. In the Gita, it is the highest wisdom and those who attain it are called *brahmavid*. "I will tell you of the wisdom that leads to immortality: the beginningless Brahman, which can be called neither being nor non-being." (13:12) This is the wisdom Sri Krishna will impart to Arjuna : "Listen and I shall explain now, Arjuna, how one who has attained perfection also attains Brahman, the supreme consummation of wisdom." (18:50)

Brahman The supreme reality underlying all life, the divine ground of existence, the impersonal Godhead. It should be noted that *Brahman* is distinct from *Brahma*, a word which also appears in the Gita and refers to God the creator.

Buddha [from *budh* "to wake up"] "The Awakened one," the title given to the sage Siddhartha Gautama Shakyamuni, after he obtained complete illumination. The Buddha lived and taught in North India during the sixth century B.C.

buddhi Understanding, intelligence; the faculty of discrimination and judgment; loosely, the "higher mind." The Gita places great importance in this faculty and warns that its loss leads one to utter destruction. (2:63)

deva A divine being, a god. It may refer to the older gods of the Vedas, or to Krishna and other divine figures.

Dhammapada "The Way of the Dharma," a fundamental Buddhist text that contains the words of the Buddha as preserved by his earliest disciples.

dharma Law, duty; the universal law which holds all life together in unity. This term, important in both Hinduism and Buddhism, is often left untranslated since no English word is equivalent.

Dharmakshetra "The field of righteousness." In the first verse of the Gita, the battle is said to be taking place at "the field of the Kurus" and "on the field of dharma." The word highlights the perception of the Gita as allegory and mystical vision.

Dhritarashtra The king of the Kurus and Duryodhana's father. He has been blind since birth and has therefore never been consecrated as king, yet he serves as de facto ruler. The *Mahabharata* war comes about in part because the line of succession has become blurred, while Dhritarashtra unfairly supports his own son Duryodhana as the next rightful ruler. The entire Bhagavad Gita is seen in a vision by Sanjaya, who then narrates what is happening to the blind king.

dhyana yoga The yoga of meditation. Also the title of chapter 6 of the Gita, which gives an insightful account of meditation in a few compact verses.

Divine Mother In India God is worshipped as the Divine Mother in many forms: Kali, Durga, Parvati, Lakshmi, and many others.

Duryodhana The oldest son of Dhritarashtra and the chief adversary of the Pandavas and Sri Krishna. At the end of the battle he is slain by Arjuna's brother Bhima.

Gita "The Song," abbreviation for Bhagavad Gita.

guna Quality; in particular, the three qualities which make up the phenomenal world of prakriti: *sattva*, law, harmony, purity, goodness; *rajas*, energy, passion; and *tamas*, inertia, ignorance, darkness. The corresponding adjectives are *sattvic, rajasic,* and *tamasic.* The Gita develops the concept of the gunas at length, and it is further developed in the later Sankhya system.

hatha yoga The *Yoga Sutras* of Patanjali, the classic text on yoga, outlines a comprehensive eightfold path, including *asanas*, or postures, as well as the training of attention, moral rules, and meditation. But the word *yoga* is widely understood today to mean health and physical fitness alone, an approach that is more rightly called hatha yoga. The Gita refers often to yoga but not in a technical way – neither in Patanjali's meaning nor in the hatha yoga meaning.

Himalaya [*hima* "snow"; *alaya* "abode"] The great mountain range which stretches across the northern border of India, important in mythology as the home of gods and sages.

Indra The Vedic god of storms and battle. In the Veda, Indra is "chief of the gods."

ishta "That which is desired," a form of God chosen for worship.
Because it is so difficult to think of God in the abstract,
in bhakti yoga a particular form of God is chosen as the
object of devotion. It is a highly personal choice and may
be one of the many manifestations, such as Rama, Krishna,
Shiva, or the Divine Mother.

jijnasu "Those with a passion to know," from an intensive form
of the verb *jna*, "to know." Sri Krishna says the *jijnasu*,
those who wish to understand life, are among those
who seek him: "Good people come to worship me for
different reasons. Some come to the spiritual life because
of suffering, some in order to understand life; some come
through a desire to achieve life's purpose, and some come
who are men and women of wisdom." (7:16)

jnana [from *jna* "to know"] Wisdom; higher knowledge. Jnana
is wisdom that penetrates beyond the world of illusion
into reality. It is a knowledge of the "beyond," as quite
distinct from intellectual knowledge of the things of
this world (that are "not beyond"), according to the
Upanishads.

jnana yoga The way of wisdom that seeks knowledge of the
formless godhead. The Gita describes this yoga in detail,
but Krishna warns Arjuna that it is very difficult for
"creatures who have a body" to seek the formless reality,
called *avyakta*, "the Unrevealed." "Yet hazardous and
slow is the path to the Unrevealed, difficult for physical
creatures to tread." (12:5) Still, Krishna praises jnana highly
and in the Gita it is not wholly separate from karma yoga
or bhakti yoga.

kama Selfish desire. Often translated as sexual desire, *kama*
can also mean any strong self-centered desire, especially
a sensory craving. Along with anger, kama is the great

enemy that is born from the guna of rajas. (3:37) Those
who overcome these two in this life live happily:
"Those who overcome the impulses of lust and anger
which arise in the body are made whole and live in
joy." (5:23)

karma [from *kri* "to do"] Action, work. Karma can also mean
former actions which will lead to results in a cause-and-
effect relationship. Karma is a recurring theme in the Gita,
and Krishna describes how Arjuna can act in the world
without being bound by karma and ignorance. Essential
to the Gita's teaching is the concept of action without
attachment to results, yet freedom cannot be achieved by
simply trying to refrain from action.

karma yoga The way of action; the path of selfless service. The
teachings on the way of action begin in chapter 3 of the
text of the Gita, "The Way of Karma Yoga," and continue
throughout the Gita as Arjuna, the representative man of
action, continues to ask questions about what it means to
act selflessly and why Krishna teaches that action is better
than renunciation.

Kauravas "The sons of Kuru," Duryodhana and his brothers,
who are the cousins and enemies of the Pandava brothers.
The Kauravas, symbolizing the forces of darkness, and the
Pandavas, symbolizing the forces of light, are two branches
of the same dynasty who face each other on the battlefield
of Kurukshetra.

Krishna ["black"; or from *krish* "to draw, to attract to oneself"]
"The Dark One" or "He who draws us to himself." The
name of a manifestation of Vishnu, the cosmic force of
goodness, who comes to earth as Krishna to reestablish
dharma. Krishna is the friend and advisor of the Pandava
brothers, especially Arjuna, to whom he reveals the

teachings of the Bhagavad Gita. He is the inner Lord, who personifies spiritual love and lives in the hearts of all beings.

krodha Anger. Anger is an important theme in the Gita, where it is one of the main obstacles to wisdom or Self-realization. In chapter 16 of the Gita, which describes the upward and the downward paths open to humanity, Krishna warns that anger is one of the gateways to hell. (16:21)

Kurukshetra "The field of the Kurus," where the *Mahabharata* battle takes place. It is north of the modern city of Delhi. The first words of the Gita are *dharmakshetre kurukshetre*, placing the exact location of the battle.

Mahabharata The name of the great Indian epic passed down, at first in an oral tradition, since perhaps the first millennium B.C. Traditionally its authorship is attributed to the sage Vyasa. The core story relates the conflict between the descendants of Pandu (the forces of light) and those of Dhritarashtra (the forces of darkness), but this vast epic contains almost limitless numbers of stories and discourses. Today, the stories and traditions of the *Mahabharata* continue to inspire the culture, art, and spiritual teachings of India.

maya Illusion; appearance, as contrasted with Reality; the creative power of God. Maya, Krishna teaches, is a powerful force, difficult to overcome. "Few see through the veil of maya. The world, deluded, does not know that I am without birth and changeless." (7:25)

moha Infatuation, delusion. Moha is born of darkness (tamas): "When tamas is dominant a person lives in darkness – slothful, confused, and easily infatuated." (14:13)

namarupa [*nama* "name"; *rupa* "form"] "Name and form," which are limitations or veils that overlay reality. It is

through namarupa that the illusion of separateness is
maintained. The Upanishads explain it:

> *As by knowing one lump of clay, dear one,*
> *We come to know all things made out of clay*
> *That they differ only in name and form,*
> *While the stuff of which all are made is clay;*
> *As by knowing one gold nugget, dear one,*
> *We come to know all things made out of gold:*
> *That they differ only in name and form,*
> *While the stuff of which all are made is gold;*
> *As by knowing one tool of iron, dear one,*
> *We come to know all things made out of iron:*
> *That they differ only in name and form,*
> *While the stuff of which all are made is iron –*
> *So through that spiritual wisdom, dear one,*
> *We come to know that all of life is one.*
> *(Chandogya 6:1.4-6)*

nirvana [*nir* "out"; *vana* "to blow"] Complete extinction of self-
will and separateness; realization of the unity of all life; the
goal of spiritual striving.

Pandavas "The sons of Pandu," Arjuna and his four brothers.
The Pandavas are in conflict with the Kauravas, who also
claim the throne of Hastinapura. The Gita is placed on the
eve of the battle that will decide this conflict, which also
symbolizes the struggle between the forces for good and
the forces of darkness.

prajna [from *jna* "to know"] Knowledge, wisdom.

prakriti The basic energy from which the mental and physical
worlds take shape; nature. Loosely, the Sankhya system
recognizes two fundamental principles: *Purusha*, the spirit,

and *prakriti*, the world.

rajas Energy, passion. One of the three *gunas*.

Rama "Prince of Joy," who was king of the ancient land of Ayodhya and the hero of the epic *Ramayana*. Like Krishna, he is an incarnation of Vishnu, who comes to earth in age after age to reestablish dharma.

Rig Veda One of the foundational scriptures of Hinduism. Like all the Vedas, it consists of hymns, rituals, and the mystic knowledge contained in the Upanishads, which are called Vedanta, the "end of the Veda."

sadhana A body of disciplines or way of life which leads to the supreme goal of Self-realization.

samadhi Mystical union with God or with the formless Brahman. A state of intense concentration in which consciousness is completely unified, withdrawn from the world, and focused within. In a famous verse, Arjuna asks Krishna to describe the person who is established in samadhi and wisdom. (2:54)

Sama Veda The Veda of songs and chants. One of the four foundational scriptures of Hinduism, received directly from divine inspiration rather than handed down by tradition.

samskara A conditioned tendency in the mind, a rigid formation in the personality. The Gita itself does not use this term, but in the commentary that established the Gita as a basic text of Vedanta, Shankara speaks of samskaras as the tendencies acquired in previous births. These impressions, or latencies, are then manifested in one's current consciousness, often leading to harmful actions and blocking the way to true wisdom.

sanatana dharma The "eternal dharma," the changeless truth underlying all religious teaching. In the Hindu tradition, it is believed that this eternal truth is revealed in the scriptures, the Vedas, and in the consciousness of illumined saints and sages.

Sanjaya King Dhritarashtra's counselor. In a vision the clairvoyant Sanjaya perceives all that is taking place on the battlefield at Kurukshetra, including the dialogue between Krishna and Arjuna, and reports it to the blind king.

Sankhya One of the six branches of Hindu philosophy developed after the Gita, though the Gita contains many of the sankhya concepts in a less systematic form. The three gunas, prominent in the Gita, are basic to Sankhya, which seeks to liberate the individual Purusha (spirit) from prakriti (mind and matter).

sattva The quality (guna) of light, law, and purity.

Shankara An Indian philosopher and mystic of the eighth century A.D. His commentary established the Gita as a principal work of Vedanta. Shankara taught a strict nondualism, with a focus on the impersonal Brahman. By Shankara's time, centuries after the Gita, the various schools of Indian philosophy were highly developed and each taught a distinct system, with lively debates between the various Hindu schools and with the followers of Buddhism and Jainism as well.

Shiva One of the principal gods of the Hindu tradition. As Brahma is called the creator and Vishnu the preserver, Shiva is the destroyer, but he is also called the conqueror of death.

shraddha Faith, belief. Many times in the Gita Krishna encourages Arjuna to have faith and says those who have faith are very dear to him. Even those who worship wrongly, if they have faith, will attain wisdom in the end.

Sri [pronounced *shree*] A title of respect originally meaning
   "auspicious" or "holy."

tamas The quality (guna) of darkness, apathy.

tat tvam asi "You are that." In the Chandogya Upanishad, the
   teacher tells his son Shvetaketu "You are that," meaning
   that the Atman (Self) within him is the same as the
   universal Brahman. For Shankara and other teachers of
   Vedanta, this is the ultimate wisdom:

   In the beginning was only Being,
   One without a second.
   Out of himself he brought forth the cosmos
   And entered into everything in it.
   There is nothing that does not come from him.
   Of everything he is the inmost Self.
   He is the truth; he is the Self supreme.
   You are that, Shvetaketu; you are that.
      (Chandogya 6:2.2-3)

upadhi An apparent limitation placed on one thing by another.
   This is a term used by Shankara, who gives the example
   of space (*akasha*) within a jar. The jar seems to contain a
   portion of the *akasha*, which of course exists both within
   and without the jar. And so the jar is an *upadhi* – when it
   is broken, the artificial limitation is no more.

Upanishads Ancient mystical documents found at the end of
   each of the Vedas. Unlike the earlier portions of the Veda,
   which focus on ritual and prayer, the Upanishads seek
   knowledge of the absolute.

Veda [from *vid* "to know"] "Knowledge"; the name of the most
   ancient Sanskrit scriptures, revered as the direct revelation

from God to the saints and sages of the past. The Vedas were composed and transmitted orally, handed down in priestly families.

Vishnu The Preserver who incarnates in age after age for the reestablishment of dharma and for the welfare of all creatures. Krishna and Rama are two of his many manifestations.

yoga [from *yuj* "to unite"] Union with God; a path or discipline which leads to a state of total integration or unity. The word *yoga* is used many times in the Gita, with several shades of meaning, including joining, method, work, union, discipline, and meditation. The Gita also frequently uses the verb *yuj* to mean "to join, yoke, prepare, or concentrate," among other meanings. It also refers to a classical school of Hindu philosophy, in which case *Yoga* is capitalized.

yuga An age or eon. In Hindu cosmology there are four yugas, representing a steady deterioration in the state of the world from age to age, until the cosmos is reborn into a new cycle of existence. We are presently living in Kali Yuga, the fourth yuga, in which dharma is weakest.

◈ Index

BOOKS BY EKNATH EASWARAN

THE CLASSICS OF INDIAN SPIRITUALITY
Easwaran's translations, with detailed introductions explaining the
cultural background and core concepts of each scripture

THE BHAGAVAD GITA

THE UPANISHADS

THE DHAMMAPADA

THE WISDOM OF INDIA
Easwaran's personal interpretations of these three scriptures

ESSENCE OF THE BHAGAVAD GITA
A Contemporary Guide to Yoga, Meditation, & Indian Philosophy

ESSENCE OF THE UPANISHADS
A Key to Indian Spirituality

ESSENCE OF THE DHAMMAPADA
The Buddha's Call to Nirvana

THE BHAGAVAD GITA FOR DAILY LIVING
Easwaran's verse-by-verse commentary, with stories, insights, and
spiritual guidance to bring the Gita's teachings into our own lives

VOLUME 1: *Chapters 1–6 The End of Sorrow*

VOLUME 2: *Chapters 7–12 Like a Thousand Suns*

VOLUME 3: *Chapters 13–18 To Love Is to Know Me*

BOOKS BY EKNATH EASWARAN

PASSAGE MEDITATION –
A COMPLETE SPIRITUAL PRACTICE
Train Your Mind, and Find a Life that Fulfills

Easwaran's classic manual is a unique source of practical spiritual support for new and experienced meditators, and gives all the instruction needed to establish a vibrant meditation practice and keep it going. In passage meditation, you focus attention on passages, or texts, drawn from all the world's traditions. You choose the passages that appeal to you, so this universal method stays fresh and inspiring, prompting you to live out your highest ideals.

Eknath Easwaran taught passage meditation to thousands of people for over forty years, including a course at the University of California, Berkeley. Meditation is supported by the mantram and six other spiritual tools to help us stay calm, kind, and focused throughout the day. This book shows how, with regular practice, we gain wisdom and vitality, and find a life that fulfills.

CONQUEST OF MIND
Take Charge of Your Thoughts and
Reshape Your Life Through Meditation

Feeling trapped by unwanted thoughts and emotions can seem an inevitable part of life. Easwaran draws on teachings from the Buddha to show how we can take charge of our thoughts and function more effectively throughout the day.

BOOKS BY EKNATH EASWARAN

GANDHI THE MAN
How One Man Changed Himself to Change the World
Easwaran gives a moving account of the turning points and choices in Gandhi's life that made him not just a great political leader but also an icon of nonviolence in the world today.

THE MANTRAM HANDBOOK
*A Practical Guide to Choosing Your Mantram
and Calming Your Mind*
Easwaran gives comprehensive instructions on how to choose and use a mantram, and explains how this spiritual discipline helps us access our deepest resources in the midst of life's problems.

GOD MAKES THE RIVERS TO FLOW
An Anthology of the World's Sacred Poetry and Prose
This is Easwaran's personal selection of passages for meditation from the Christian, Buddhist, Hindu, Jewish, Taoist, Sufi, and Native American traditions. Detailed background notes and supporting material are included.

ORIGINAL GOODNESS
A Commentary on the Beatitudes
Original goodness is Easwaran's phrase for the spark of divinity hidden in every one of us, regardless of our personal liabilities or past mistakes. Easwaran shows how this spark can ener-gize our lives - beginning with a simple method of meditation that gradually removes the conditioning that hides our native goodness.

BOOKS BY EKNATH EASWARAN

WORDS TO LIVE BY
Daily Inspiration for Spiritual Living
With a short reading for each day of the year, Easwaran inspires
us with wisdom to guide us in our daily lives. Each reading is
introduced by a quotation from one the world's great philosophers, poets, saints, and sages.

STRENGTH IN THE STORM
Transform Stress, Live in Balance and Find Peace of Mind
We can't always control what life sends us, but we can choose
how we respond. With stories and practical spiritual techniques,
Easwaran shows how to find balance, peace, and wisdom by
learning to steady our minds.

TAKE YOUR TIME
The Wisdom of Slowing Down
Through stories, insights, and step-by-step advice, Easwaran
shows us how to calm our minds. When the mind is unhur-
ried, we are patient, kind, and focused, ready to respond to what
really matters amidst the clamor of a busy day.

TIMELESS WISDOM
Passages for Meditation from the World's Saints and Sages
A compact, portable collection of inspirational passages that
represent all the world's major mystical traditions, selected
from Easwaran's *God Makes the Rivers to Flow* and including
nine new passages.

Blue Mountain
Center of Meditation

The Blue Mountain Center of Meditation publishes Eknath Easwaran's books, videos, and audio recordings, and offers retreats and online programs on his eight-point program of passage meditation.

For more information and resources, please visit: www.bmcm.org

The Blue Mountain Center of Meditation
Box 256, Tomales, California 94971 USA
Telephone: +1 707 878 2369
Toll-free in the US: 800 475 2369
Email: info@bmcm.org